TIME FOR A PARTY

time for a  P arty

BY RUTH BRENT

McGRAW-HILL BOOK COMPANY, INC.

THE

COMPLETE

HOME PARTY

BOOK

NEW YORK   TORONTO   LONDON

Library of Congress Catalog Card Number: 57–11841

First Edition
Second Printing

acknowledgments

My thanks to all the dear friends in many parts of the world who have shared their recipes and contributed party ideas for this book.

I'm most grateful to the editors of *Good Housekeeping* magazine for allowing me to reprint the parties which were first used in their magazine.

My gratitude to B. Altman and Co., who made it possible to photograph the table settings illustrating some of the parties in this book, and my particular thanks to Mr. Daniel Danoff, who helped design and assemble them.

I should also like to thank Mr. William Syzdek, "photographer extraordinaire," for his fine work and assistance.

Ruth Brent

For Mother, Dad, and "My Best Beau"

I HOW TO PLAN PARTIES

II PARTIES FOR ALL OCCASIONS

COFFEES AND LUNCHEONS

RECEPTIONS AND COCKTAIL PARTIES

DINNERS AND BUFFET SUPPERS

Contents

part I

how to plan parties

Entertaining with a flair

My purpose in writing this book is to show how *you* can give wonderful parties even if you've never given one before; and what's more, you'll have wonderful fun doing it.

This can be accomplished by means of the Party Plan, pages 7–10, which lists each step from the time you issue the invitations to the moment you light your candles and call your guests to dinner. I've tried to explain each step clearly, just as if I were sitting at your kitchen table and we were planning the party together.

Is there anything more gay and heartwarming than a houseful of laughing, happy people? Nothing gives a couple a greater feeling of accomplishment than the realization that their friends are always completely relaxed in their home and look forward eagerly to every party there. It really does something for a host and hostess to hear guests laughing heartily at a joke, or singing their hearts out around the piano, or simply sitting around the fire telling stories or relating fascinating experiences they have had.

The gracious custom of entertaining in the home has had a great upswing in recent years. This is due in part to the creative ideas of architects in designing den-kitchens, outdoor living areas, indoor rotisseries, and fireplaces. Let's not let these innovations go to waste. Your home reflects your family's personality, and you can give your friends great pleasure by sharing it with them.

A home is at its gayest when there are frequent parties for both adults and children, and children have opportunities to become better adapted and more self-assured when they can both entertain friends and be entertained elsewhere. Included in the book are parties for children and teen-agers with some very unusual and gay ideas.

Gracious and competent hostesses are made, not born. Entertaining is an art which, like any other accomplishment, can be developed with practice. After you have mastered the easy parties described in the book, I believe you'll enjoy trying such

sophisticated ideas as Shishkebab Cooked in the Fireplace, the Japanese Sukiyaki Dinner, or the New England Clambake.

The book is divided into two parts:

1. Information which will be valuable to you in planning your own parties: (I think you will find the chapter On Being a Good Host and Hostess particularly helpful.)

2. Complete parties following certain themes: These supply you with menus, recipes, invitations, table settings, methods of serving, schedules, favors, and games. I feel that a detailed plan for one party, such as the Bride's First Buffet Supper on page 151, will be more valuable to you than would an entire book of general suggestions. If you would like to learn how to entertain with a flair, this is the book for you.

INTRODUCING THE PARTY PLAN

First of all, I should like to introduce the Party Plan. It will be referred to repeatedly and I hope, as you become familiar with it, that you will become as affectionately attached to it as I am.

Instead of countless little scraps of paper (so easily mislaid) listing your guests, menu, shopping lists, and errands, the Party Plan enables you to keep all details in order in one place, and allows room to check off errands as you complete them.

Although it was designed to help young brides with their first parties, the usefulness of the Plan has been extended far beyond its original purpose. Picture the advantages of having a permanent record of your entertaining:

- You will have a record of your guests, which will enable you to determine easily whether or not you are fulfilling all your social obligations.

- You can avoid serving one menu to the same guests more than once.

- When you have given a certain type of party once, it is easy to give it again for different groups of guests. Your recipes and shopping lists are all made out, the table-setting and serving equipment you will need is recorded, the manner in which you are going to serve has been worked out, and your party-day schedule is there.

PARTY PLAN

TYPE OF PARTY .... DATE .... TIME From ...... to ......

GUEST LIST	MENU

RECIPES

In this section either write or type out the recipes, or make a note of the cookbook and page number where they may be found. In addition make a note of the serving dish you will use for each item on the menu, and how you intend arranging and garnishing it.

SHOPPING LISTS

GROCERY LIST		MISCELLANEOUS LIST	
		CIGARETTES	
		FLOWERS and/or OTHER MATERIAL	
		FOR CENTERPIECE	
		CANDLES	
		MINTS	
		PRIZES FOR GAMES	
		EQUIPMENT FOR GAMES	
		COCKTAIL NAPKINS	
		PLACE CARDS	
		FAVORS	

DESCRIPTION OF TABLE

TABLE: TYPE AND LOCATION

CLOTH:

NAPKINS:

CHINA:

GLASSWARE:

CANDLEHOLDERS:

CENTERPIECE:

SERVING DISHES:

HOW ARE YOU GOING TO SERVE?

ENTERTAINMENT

Description of games, contests, sing song or other entertainment, if any. List the prizes which will be given.

Many hostesses build their reputations on just one type of party. One couple we know gives superb barbecues—outdoors in summer, indoors at the fireplace in winter. Another couple has become known for the Sunday Punch Brunch. I have my favorite too: I adore giving a New England Clambake, and have given it so often that it no longer requires any effort.

So work out one party at a time, and give it for several different groups until you can manage it easily. Then when you want to try your wings again, work out the next Party Plan.

If you have help, the Party Plan is a wonderful convenience to hostess and maid alike. It is much easier for the maid if she can refer to written instructions than if she must remember oral ones. Once the Party Plan is made out completely, the maid should not have to consult the hostess again, because even the table setting is described in detail, and the check list for either a buffet or seated meal is given.

Entertaining isn't easy for anyone; it takes work. However, it is usually not the actual work involved which prevents the inexperienced hostess from giving parties, but either lack of confidence or lack of organization and the fear of forgetting important details.

It's true that there are innumerable details involved in giving a party, but many of them require only a moment or two, so please don't be discouraged by the length of the list. In addition, some of the items listed won't be necessary for your particular party; in that case draw a line through them.

There is one secret which all successful hostesses know. Everything must be done in advance so that at the time of the party, the hostess will be as relaxed as any of her guests. She should be able to look forward to the evening with pleasure, in the expectation of having a wonderful time at her own party. The trick to make it all seem easy is

CHECK-OFF LIST

TWO OR THREE WEEKS AHEAD:

Consult with your husband, your guest list, menu, other plans.
If you are going to have help with your party, engage your sitter, cateress, bartender.
Invite guests.
Plan menu.
Plan entertainment if you expect to play games.

SEVERAL DAYS AHEAD:

Shop for groceries.
Check clothing which you are going to wear.
Make up everything possible ahead of time, such as dressings, frozen dessert, etc.
Check your linen. Press if necessary.
Polish silver, china, glassware.
Have small tables ready to set up after guests have served themselves (if you are having a buffet).
Do you need to borrow anything?

THE DAY BEFORE:

Clean house.
Wrap prizes and assemble equipment for games.
Set your table.
Get out your serving dishes and serving forks and spoons.
Plan on having candles somewhere in the living room as well as in the dining room.
Other errands:

CHECK-OFF LIST FOR BUFFET TABLE:	CHECK-OFF LIST FOR SEATED DINNER:
Cloth	Cloth or mats
Napkins	Centerpiece
Plates	Candles (approx. 1 per person)
Silver	Napkins
Salt and pepper shakers (well filled)	Plates
Serving forks and spoons	Silver
Serving dishes, chafing dishes, etc.	Water goblets and wine glasses, if desired
Centerpiece	Salt and pepper shakers
Candles	Serving forks and spoons
Water goblets on serving table	Serving dishes
Cups and saucers on side table	Cigarette urns, trays, matches
Coffee service on side table. (Sugar bowl and cream pitcher well filled)	Butter plates
	Cups and saucers on tray with silver service, on side table or in living room, or placed in front of hostess. Cream and sugar.
	Place cards, if desired

Use this space for Seating Plan or Chart of Buffet Table.

JOBS FOR YOUR BEST BEAU:

If cocktails are being served, ask him to check supply.
Set up a small bar on a table in living room or somewhere nearby. (For small, informal parties, a sign saying SELF SERVICE BAR is a great help to the host.)
Order or make ice cubes the day before.
An open fireplace cleaned out and ready to go is a joy. (We do not recommend your suggesting this just before the party.)

PARTY DAY

The following plan is a sample one. It will be advisable for you to make up your own schedule according to your needs.

A.M.   Prepare salad ingredients and store in refrigerator.
Butter the rolls or bread.
Put fresh cigarettes in containers.
Set out additional ashtrays, lighters, coasters.
Select phonograph records.
Arrange centerpiece.
Tack up menu in convenient location.
Make list of jobs for caterers if any.
Remove frozen foods from freezer.

P.M.   Rest for an hour or two if possible.

4 P.M.   Dress.

5 P.M.   Inspect the bathroom. Set out Kleenex, fresh soap, extra bathroom tissue, face powder, individual lipsticks, in several shades.

5:15   Light fire in fireplace.

5:30   Porch light on.
Set out snack tray.

5:45   Start record player. Gay, light music, soft.
Light candles in living room. Have lamplight, no strong overhead lights.
Relax, and look forward eagerly to having your friends with you in your home. Don't forget -- they are all looking forward with pleasure to your party.

6:00   Guests start arriving. Direct them to the room set aside for their coats. As soon as they are seated, offer them a cigarette, and a cocktail if you are serving cocktails. Otherwise clam juice or fruit juice are always acceptable. The main thing is, offer them *something*. It serves to break the first formality which sometimes occurs.

6:30   Start oven. Heat your main dish.

7:00   Make coffee. (And make plenty.)

7:15   Heat rolls or bread.
Set out cream, ice water, butter.

7:30   Set food on table. Have you taken **everything** from refrigerator?
Light candles and call your guests to dinner.

8:30   Coffee and liqueurs if desired, in the living room, followed by games and/or singing.
Flash pictures of the party are fun to have as souvenirs.

REMARKS: *Fill out a Party Plan each time you entertain and file it away for future use.*

to plan your party, step by step, before you issue one invitation. Then you need only carry out all the little tasks listed on the schedule and you can't fail to have a successful party.

USE OF THE PARTY PLAN

You will be able to use the first three pages of the Party Plan just as they stand. The fourth page, here at your left, was written simply as a guide for you to follow. It will be necessary for you to make up your own schedule, depending on the type of party you are planning, the time set for it, et cetera. For your own convenience, write down the tasks to be completed on the day of the party, coordinate the cooking schedule so that all your food will be ready at the proper time, judge what time the coffee should be made, salads prepared, and so forth. Paste or staple your Party Day schedule to the Party Plan so that you will have the information at hand if you decide to repeat it.

A note of explanation here: the host and hostess have planned to attend a football game with friends whom they are going to bring home with them for an informal supper afterward. The party is so planned that there will be a minimum of last-minute preparation.

PARTY PLAN

TYPE OF PARTY *Mexican Supper* DATE *Jan. 20th* TIME From *5.30* to *?*

GUEST LIST	MENU
The Duplantis	Frosty Tequila Cocktails
	Mexican Broad Beans and Pepitas
	(nibblers)
The Welch's	Mary's Easy Tamale Pie
	Guacamole Salad
The Stacys	Natilla
(host and hostess)	(Custard with Caramel Sauce)
	Coffee

RECIPES

Frosty Tequila Cocktails - "Exotic Drink Book" Page 129

Mary's Easy Tamale Pie "Time for a Party" Page 76

Guacamole Salad   "Time for a Party" Page 76

Natilla - "Favorite Recipes from the United Nations" Page 58

Special Instructions :

  Tamale Pie - Make two to allow for seconds
            Use bake - and - serve casseroles

  Guacamole Salad - Cut each avocado in half, remove
  pit, arrange on a bed of salad greens on
  large platter. Sprinkle sliced green onions on
  avocado. Arrange wedges of tomato and
  egg around edge. Guests apply dressing.

  Natilla - Serve in sherbet dishes on dessert plate.

SHOPPING LISTS

GROCERY LIST		MISCELLANEOUS LIST	
Limes	*Avocados*	CIGARETTES	*Yes*
Pepitas	*Tomatoes*	FLOWERS and/or OTHER MATERIAL FOR CENTERPIECE	*Yes*
Chopped beef	*Eggs*		
Onions	*Green onions*	CANDLES	*Yes*
Green pepper	*Milk*	MINTS	*No*
Tomato sauce	*Cornmuffin mix*	PRIZES FOR GAMES	*No*
Garlic		EQUIPMENT FOR GAMES	*No*
Kidney beans		COCKTAIL NAPKINS	*Yes*
Salad greens		PLACE CARDS	*Yes*
Mexican broad beans	*Tequila*	FAVORS	*No*

DESCRIPTION OF TABLE

Mexican national colors – red, white and green

TABLE: TYPE AND LOCATION *Dining room table*

CLOTH: *made of cotton yard goods. Black background with a Mexican-Indian print in red, white and green.*

NAPKINS: *Red cotton*

CHINA: *Small white platters with fluted edge; cups and saucers*

GLASSWARE: *Bright green Mexican goblets*

CANDLEHOLDERS: *Green peppers hollowed out; white candles*

CENTERPIECE: *Red and green peppers, white onions, green leaves.*

SERVING DISHES: *Tamale pie in casserole ; salad on white platter.*

HOW ARE YOU GOING TO SERVE? *Place the tamale pie, salad, dressing and small platters on the buffet. Guests serve themselves then find their places at the table. Dessert and coffee service will be on a tea cart near the hostess.*

ENTERTAINMENT

Description of games, contests, sing song or other entertainment, if any. List the prizes which will be given.

Primarily good conversation. In addition, a long-playing record of beautiful Mexican music would be pleasant.

CHECK-OFF LIST

Two or Three Weeks Ahead:

Consult with your husband, your guest list, menu, other plans. ✔

If you are going to have help with your party, engage your sitter, cateress, bartender. *no*

Invite guests. ✔

Plan menu. ✔

Plan entertainment if you expect to play games. *no*

Several Days Ahead:

Shop for groceries. ✔

Check clothing which you are going to wear. ✔

Make up everything possible ahead of time, such as dressings, frozen dessert, etc. ✔

Check your linen. Press if necessary. ✔

Polish silver, china, glassware. ✔

Have small tables ready to set up after guests have served themselves (if you are having a buffet). *no*

Do you need to borrow anything? *Album of Mexican music*

The Day Before:

Clean house. ✔

Wrap prizes and assemble equipment for games. *no*

Set your table. ✔

Get out your serving dishes and serving forks and spoons. ✔

Plan on having candles somewhere in the living room as well as in the dining room. ✔

Other errands: *Beauty Shop Friday at 1*

Check-Off List for Buffet Table:

Cloth

Napkins

Plates

Silver

Salt and pepper shakers (well filled)

Serving forks and spoons

Serving dishes, chafing dishes, etc.

Centerpiece

Candles

Water goblets on serving table

Cups and saucers on side table

Coffee service on side table. (Sugar bowl and cream pitcher well filled)

Check-Off List for Seated Dinner:

Cloth or mats ✔

Centerpiece ✔

Candles (approx. 1 per person) ✔

Napkins ✔

Plates ✔

Silver ✔

Water goblets and wine glasses, if desired ✔

Salt and pepper shakers ✔

Serving forks and spoons ✔

Serving dishes ✔

Cigarette urns, trays, matches ✔

Butter plates *no*

Cups and saucers on tray with silver service, on side table or in living room, or placed in front of hostess. Cream and sugar. ✔

Place cards, if desired ✔

Use this space for Seating Plan or Chart of Buffet Table.

Senor Welch   Senora Duplantis

Senora Stacy   Senor Stacy

Senor Duplantis   Senora Welch

Jobs for Your Best Beau:

If cocktails are being served, ask him to check supply.

Set up a small bar on a table in living room or somewhere nearby. (For small, informal parties, a sign saying *SELF SERVICE BAR* is a great help to the host.)

Order or make ice cubes the day before.

An open fireplace cleaned out and ready to go is a joy. (We do not recommend your suggesting this just before the party.)

PARTY DAY

A.M. Prepare salad ingredients.*Make lime dressing,
*tamale pie filling, and *dessert, and store
all of them in refrigerator.
Put fresh cigarettes in containers.
Set out additional ashtrays, lighters, coasters.
Place Mexican album near record player.
Arrange centerpiece.
Tack up menu in convenient location.

12.15 Dress, then tidy up the bathroom.

1.30 Leave for game

5.30 Arrive home from game with guests.
Turn oven to 425°.
Light candles in living room.
Light fire in fireplace.
Start record player.
Spread the topping on casserole.

5.45 Pop it into oven and rejoin guests.
Bring in nibblers in bowls to accompany
cocktails.

6.15 Make coffee and salad.

6.30 Fill water glasses, light candles, set food
on buffet, call guests to dinner.

* These items could be made the day before.

REMARKS: *Fill out a Party Plan each time you entertain and file it away for future use.*

on being a

Good host

and hostess

Since practically the whole success of a party depends on the host and hostess, I've devoted a substantial amount of space to this chapter.

PLANNING THE PARTY

I am not trying to make entertaining seem a formidable undertaking, because it isn't. Though you will probably be unable to carry out all these suggestions on your first party, if you keep them in mind and include a few more each time you entertain, they will soon become automatic; before you know it you may even gain the reputation of being the best hostess in town. Few of us seek this distinction, but there's no denying that it is music to our ears to know that people love visiting us, and that invitations to our homes are coveted.

As Betty Betz says in her book:

"Unless you plan to be a hermit and live in a cave the rest of your life, the sooner you learn the art of being a good host and hostess the better."

In making your first plans, decide what kind of party you most enjoy giving, how many guests your home can comfortably accommodate, how much money you want to spend, and what your entertaining obligations are.

You may find it easier to give two supper parties for six than one for twelve, and most guests prefer a relatively small party. There are other advantages too: you may have china for only six or eight; for a small group you can serve a sit-down dinner which is more comfortable than a buffet; there is little confusion during a small party; and it is easier to entertain only a few people gracefully, particularly if you must be a combination waitress-cook-hostess.

Consider carefully what your guests most enjoy, and not your own preferences. Your first object should be to give your guests a wonderfully happy evening. On the other hand try to be a little original in your choice of a menu and in your table decorations. Don't copy your friends' parties.

CHECK-OFF LISTS

The Party Plan form, page 7 to page 10, is the one I fill out each time I plan a party. You will notice it is composed of:

1. Spaces for guest list, menu, recipes, grocery list, miscellaneous list;
2. A space for description of the linen, china, glassware, and other equipment you will use on your table;
3. Spaces marked "How are you going to serve?" and "What entertainment are you planning?";
4. Check-off lists reading:
   Two or three weeks ahead;
   Several days ahead;
   The day before;
5. Check-off lists for buffet table and for seated meals, and a space for your seating plan or chart of buffet table;
6. A space which I know you'll love: Jobs for your best beau;
7. The last page is devoted to Party Day— first the morning chores, then the afternoon ones. (This page was meant to be only a guide for you. It will be advisable for you to make out your own schedule according to your needs.)

Go over these lists carefully to make sure that nothing is forgotten. Do as much as possible ahead of time. File your party plan for future use; the details, guest list, and menu will be invaluable for future entertaining.

GUEST LIST

Make up your guest list of people you think will enjoy and be interested in one another. Be a little selfish too, and invite people you personally like, those who give you confidence, those you know will enjoy and appreciate your efforts. Guests with a gift for small talk are a great asset, as are those who have a good sense of humor in conversing or the equally important talent of listening.

However, it is wise to include a new couple or two every once in a while. The exchange of new ideas makes conversation more stimulating. It is wise to invite people who have common interests, but not rivals; one celebrity at a party works out better than two. And to avoid making everyone uncomfortable don't invite two persons who are feuding to the same party.

If you invite a person either older or younger than the general age level, it is a kindness to include another guest of the same age. If you are entertaining a single woman, it will make the party more pleasant for her if you invite an unattached man.

INVITATIONS

Whether you extend your invitations by telephone or mail, allow at least ten days. During the holiday season, get them out two to three weeks in advance to avoid disappointment.

When inviting a couple to an affair, the hostess extends the invitation to the wife. When inviting an unattached man, the hostess drops him a note or calls him personally.

State clearly the place, time, and occasion. If the party is in honor of someone, don't keep that fact in the dark. If gifts are to be given, let everyone know. It is embarrassing to be the only one who has come empty-handed.

Be specific about what is known in military parlance as the "Uniform of the Day." You might say, "it's to be an informal party.

I believe the girls will wear cocktail dresses, and the men business suits." Or, "We're going to have the barbecue outside, so the girls will probably wear cotton dresses and the men slacks and sports shirts. (And woe betide the girl who neglects to pass on this information to her husband, who, on a warm summer evening, is the only one in a suit while all the others are lounging comfortably in sports clothes.)

If your home is difficult to find and a guest has not been there before, it is thoughtful to give clear directions on how to find it, preferably in writing.

If you plan to play bridge, canasta, or poker, or expect to watch a certain program on television, I believe it is a good idea to mention it in the invitation.

MENU

This is more fully covered in the chapter entitled "Menu Planning." However, I'd like to mention the following important suggestions:

1. Provide good tasty food, not necessarily elaborate, but plentiful (enough for seconds) and displayed attractively. It is better to provide an abundance of simple fare than to skimp on more costly dishes. Two courses are ample for a buffet:

Main Course   *Hot Rolls*

Dessert   *Coffee*

For a seated dinner you might plan three courses:

Soup or Salad

Main Course

Dessert   *Coffee*

(It is far better to serve a few courses well than many courses with confusion.)

2. Particularly for your first parties, plan to serve food you can prepare without effort, with which you are entirely familiar.

3. It is fun to experiment with exotic and different menus, but the hostess should test them before serving them at a party. After you've really perfected, for instance, the traditional party fare of turkey or ham or chicken, how about branching out next time by serving shishkebabs or a Chinese dinner? The challenge and results will be worth the effort. Guests love the unexpected.

4. If possible, plan something which can be prepared the day before.

5. If you decide to serve such food as lobster, shrimp, oysters, or roquefort cheese, either make sure ahead of time that your guests like it or prepare an alternate dish.

6. For a buffet, plan a menu which can be managed with the fork alone (unless you equip your guests with lap trays).

7. When you decide on your menu, picture the way the food will look on your table, on your platters and vegetable dishes, and on your china. What you serve will depend to some extent on the equipment you have —that is, both serving dishes and cooking vessels.

8. Your food will decorate your table as much as or more than your centerpiece, so make it look pretty both in color and in garnishing. Even one bright spot of color makes a great difference.

9. Every recipe book stresses this point: serve hot things *hot*, and cold things *cold*.

10. Another way to entertain is to cook all or part of your meal before the admiring eyes of your guests; for example, cook steaks in the fireplace. One advantage in this plan is that in the group there may be someone who wants to get in the act and prove his prowess at this art. He or she can take over this responsibility from you, so be prepared to wrap a large barbecue apron around this delightful person.

THE SETTING

Although we may not be able to provide a pretentious setting (or even want to), we can provide a cheerful, gay one. The atmosphere of a successful party is hard to define or explain. However each of these things has its effect:

> Candlelight   A flickering fire
> Soft music   The fragrance of flowers
> Soft lamplight

These things *do* have an effect on guests— and the hostess who just doesn't bother is depriving her guests of a lot of pleasure in not taking advantage of them. But almost more important, she is depriving herself of that feeling of confidence and wellbeing that a party-bedecked home can inspire. Each of these things helps to say "welcome"; they compliment each guest by saying that the hostess cherishes the honor of his presence. He is expected, and preparations have been made for his pleasure.

When you are prettying up your home for the party, don't neglect the entrance hall. In addition to a good bright light, and a place set aside for wraps, plan to have a vase of seasonal greens or a bouquet on the hall table.

A small bouquet also adds a touch of glamour to your bedroom. Many hostesses even have plants or flowers in the bathroom.

In addition to these things, the furniture arrangement in the room contributes to the party's success. If you are entertaining six or fewer, it is best to arrange the chairs to form a cozy group, so that you can all share in one conversation.

A small table between each two guests is a convenience, not only if you are serving a buffet supper, but as a place for cocktail glasses, ashtrays, and before-dinner nibblers.

For a stand-up affair such as a reception, cocktail party, or tea, it is wise to push furniture back against the walls to leave as much space as possible in the center of the room.

Large ashtrays (preferably plain glass ones), lighters, and matches should be placed here and there, as well as coasters for your cocktails. One or two brands of cigarettes are sufficient, as guests usually bring their own.

A bright porch light helps direct guests to your home and gives the pleasant reassurance that they are expected.

We hope, too, that you'll remember to clear the sidewalks and steps of snow in the wintertime; in the summertime clear the walk of cut grass and remove all such obstacles as toys or bicycles. One other thing —air the house thoroughly before the party so it will be fresh and free of cooking odors.

CHECK-OFF LIST *Fifteen minutes before the party*

Equipment and prizes ready for games if any?

Small tables set up convenient to chairs in a conversational circle?

Overhead lights off?

Table completely set?

Cocktail ingredients ready? Cocktail napkins? Coasters?

Cigarettes in containers, and matches and ashtrays nearby?

Has everything been taken from the freezer?

Is bathroom in order?

Is fire lighted?

Are porch light and entrance light on?

Are snack bowls filled and set out?

Record player providing soft music?

Candles lighted in the living room?

Camera and flash ready for taking pictures?

WELCOMING THE GUESTS

APPEARANCE AND PARTY MOOD OF THE HOST AND HOSTESS

As the hour for the party approaches, you should have a feeling of happy anticipation, as you would at that magic moment just before the curtain rises on the first act of a play.

If you have planned carefully, most of the work is behind you, and you are entitled to have as good a time as anyone else at the party, if not a better one.

We hope that you have been able to rest for an hour before dressing in your prettiest hostess costume so that you will be fresh and completely relaxed. It is important for your peace of mind that you be well dressed and well groomed, so give some thought to this. The host too, of course, should be immaculate and dressed in his best.

By greeting your guests at the door with a warm smile and a sincere handshake or hug, you are showing them that you are delighted to see them—an assurance that will give them a glow of pleasure. By being gracious and serene, you can assure them that you expect to enjoy yourself, and you expect them to do the same. Your joyous party mood shows that you have everything under control, and have not a care in the world. (No one likes the feeling that the hostess has gone to a lot of trouble to entertain him. The trick for the hostess to develop is to make it all seem very casual—as if it were no trouble at all.)

It is only natural to reflect the mood of the persons we are with, so the cheerfulness or (heaven forbid) the worried gloom of a host and hostess are quickly reflected in the manner of the guests. So, even if you're not absolutely carefree when your first guests arrive, *pretend you are*. All you need do is to be your own sweet, natural self; your guests will take over from there.

Don't apologize for anything. It just embarrasses people, and what may seem less than perfect to you will probably not even be noticed by others.

THE HOST HELPS

The success of a party depends on the host too. Here are some of the things he can do to make everything run smoothly:

Help with the introductions

See that no one is stranded

Help keep the conversation in interesting channels, and listen attentively to others

See that guests are supplied with drinks if they want them

Proffer cigarettes and light them

Empty ashtrays occasionally

Be gracious and courteous to all (and it doesn't hurt a bit to tell the girls how nice they look)

One last thing—allow yourself plenty of time to get ready. It is disconcerting to guest and hostess alike if you haven't quite finished dressing, or are frantically rushing around doing things which should have been done earlier. However, if you do find yourself in this position, leave such tasks as putting out cigarettes, which won't be particularly noticeable or which, if the guest is a close friend, she can help with. Most people don't mind lending a hand, but are, in fact, glad to if they happen to be the first ones there.

THE WELCOME AT THE DOOR

The small party. Welcome each guest with affection and enthusiasm. Shake hands with each one as he enters. Naturally you will be smiling if you greet the guests yourself. If a maid has this duty, she should be encouraged to smile and say "Good evening, sir" or "Good evening, madam," in a pleasant manner. Then she should help guests with their wraps or direct them to the room set aside for wraps.

If you are in a tiny apartment and must use a hall closet for guests' wraps, at least make room for them, and have hangers available; also set aside a space on the shelf for hats. For a really large party, it might be best to rent a coat rack and place it either in the hall or in a bedroom.

The large party. The host and hostess will probably receive in the living room so that they may greet guests as they arrive and bid them farewell as they leave without running back and forth to the door. In this way, too, they are able to keep an eye on the serving of food and drinks, and to visit with guests.

If this arrangement is used, there must be either a maid or a member of the family or close friend (preferably one who knows most of the guests expected) at the door. (Many of our friends have their young son or daughter take on this task and it works out very well indeed. Young people usually like to be in the act, too, and to be an important part of the party.) I should think that any boy or girl over ten years of age might be given this responsibility. All they need do is smile and say, "I'm Lynne Diane. Won't you leave your wraps in the bedroom to your left?" After this has been taken care of, she will direct them to the room where her mother and father are receiving. As far as possible the latter should remain in plain sight so that guests do not have to wander around trying to find them.

Here again, host and hostess must give a really warm greeting to guests and introduce them to at least one nearby group.

INTRODUCTIONS

When giving a small party, you should introduce each guest as he arrives to everyone present.

When giving a large party, it is best to introduce him to one group only. From then on other guests are expected to introduce him as the occasion arises, or he will introduce himself. On no account introduce him around a room, then feel your obligations are over and leave him stranded. Your responsibility is to see that he is at ease as part of a group before you leave on other hostess duties.

Do be careful to pronounce each name clearly, and if possible go on with an explanatory remark, such as "Mr. Jahn is a professor at City College," or, "I've been wanting you two to meet—both of you being so interested in Little Theater work," or something of the kind. This immediately gives your guests something other than the weather with which to start the conversation.

In introducing a person to a group, avoid interrupting if a story is in process. Wait until it is finished, or at least until there is a pause.

If you have invited older persons to your party, or out-of-town guests, you should make a particular effort to introduce them to as many people as possible, and see that they have a good time. Often it is advisable to ask a close friend to assume this responsibility as it will be necessary at times for you to be out of the room.

So that introductions will go smoothly, make up guest lists for both you and your husband beforehand. Prop them up on your respective dressers, and refer to them as you are dressing. You'll be surprised how much it will help you later on when you are introducing a roomful of people.

It is a thoughtful gesture to make another guest list for a guest-of-honor, with a short explanatory comment about those he or she doesn't know.

THE PARTY IS UNDER WAY

THE CUP THAT CHEERS

The most important thing to learn in being a hospitable host and hostess is to offer a guest *something* as soon as he or she sits down. It may be a cocktail, a glass of fruit juice, a cup of tea, or a piece of candy, depending on the time of day. There is something about sharing a refreshing drink, alcoholic or not, which immediately puts both hostess and guest at ease. We have occasionally attended parties where no one is offered a cocktail until all guests have assembled. The early ones have to wait for the late ones, and there is sometimes an uncomfortable tense period before the party gets under way. If you are serving manhattans, martinis, or daiquiris, it is a good idea to have one shakerful made up and ready to go. If your party gets off to a good start during the first few minutes, you can relax from then on; it will "give" itself and go forward under its own momentum.

A cocktail shaker is especially convenient at parties as you can refill glasses as necessary without taking them back to the bar.

A supply of ginger ale, cola, or fruit juice should be included so that those who do not care for alcoholic drinks can have a substitute. Clam juice and tomato juice are popular too. A refreshing summertime drink is pineapple juice with a sprig of mint in it. Cranberry juice cocktails are festive too.

One mistake that many hosts and hostesses make is to extend the cocktail hour too long before dinner. If you have invited your guests for 7, you should plan to have dinner at 8. Too many cocktails will lessen rather than stimulate gaiety.

Don't be insistent and beg a guest to "have just one more," and if he asks for a half drink, give him just that.

Another must is *plenty of ice*; if you have a freezer you can store a quantity in waxed paper bags or plastic containers beforehand. Otherwise it would be wise to order some extra from your ice dealer.

DURING THE PARTY

You should, if at all possible, visit with each of your guests at some time during the party. This is particularly important with regard to elderly people, friends from out of town, and shy people. See that the latter are included in conversation and games if any. Many times you can help to put them at ease by asking them to help you in some way, such as passing hors d'oeuvres or cigarettes.

The majority of people are flattered to be asked to help at your party. In this day of little household help the hostess can't be expected to do everything herself. Having a guest perform even such a small chore as passing cigarettes or emptying ashtrays can be a great help.

Either the hostess or the host should be in the room with the guests at all times.

Ensure the comfort of your guests by maintaining a moderate temperature if possible, not letting the rooms get too hot or too cold.

Although ashtrays should be emptied once or twice during the evening, don't make this activity obvious by doing it too often; maybe your best beau would take on this task. That silent butler you received as a wedding gift will come in handy here.

Although it is a temptation to take your friends on a tour of inspection through your new home, don't do it at the expense of other guests left alone in the living room.

Avoid separating groups as much as possible. Sometimes, of course, with a large number of people, of necessity you have to route them to various locations in your home, but I think it is gayer if you can keep all your guests in close proximity.

You're proud of your pets and love them dearly, but unfortunately this feeling is sometimes not shared by others. Some are allergic to cat and dog fur, some are afraid of animals, and some just don't like them. So if it is at all practical to put them in confinement for a few hours, your guests may be happier. Another hazard—pets, in their enthusiasm, may jump on party dresses or ruin nylons.

Try to discourage guests from separating into groups of men huddled on one side of the room and women on the other. Many times it can be done in a light manner by saying, "Come on, Ann and Betty, let's break up the football session over here." It is ordinarily much more fun for the conversation to be of a general nature, and more satisfying to everyone.

And please forget kitchen clean-up duties until guests have gone. Don't spoil the party mood.

ENTERTAINMENT

CONVERSATION. You can look the world over and never find better entertainment than good conversation. At times it seems to be a lost art, and what a pity it is.

Keep conversation flowing in interesting channels. If one of your guests starts on a tiresome monologue of her ailments or maid troubles, the host or hostess must save the situation. At the first pause, one or the other could break in and say "That reminds me of a funny maid story" or "Have you heard of the wonderful medical experiments they are conducting?" In other words direct the conversation into a more general discussion first, then try to veer away from the objectionable topic altogether.

And most important, avoid purely "woman talk" or "man talk." The baby's formula may be of extreme interest to the young mother, but it seldom interests others. However, you must courteously wait for a break in the conversation before introducing a new topic which you hope will be of interest to all.

There are so many fascinating topics which interest and concern all of us that it seems a pity to get into these conversational ruts that happen so often. One habit that both a hostess and guest could well develop is to make a list of several interesting or amusing things that have happened recently either to you or to someone you've read about. Also other interesting bits of news. Store them in the back of your mind, then pull them out of your hat when the time comes. This is much easier than to desperately try to think of something when that dreadful awkward pause occurs. Sometimes one fascinating topic will keep a group extremely interested for hours.

If you are entertaining people from out of town try to avoid conversations of a strictly home-town theme, which interest only local people.

Of interest to the majority of people are such subjects as:

World affairs	Personal adventures
Politics	Progress in science
Current books, plays,	New inventions
movies, television	Education
Trips	

Also of interest though morbid in feeling are:

Disasters	Crimes and mysteries
Accidents	Supernatural tales

Amusing and interesting personal experiences should probably head the list. Try, however, to avoid having one person take over the conversation. By asking questions of other guests, you can usually draw everyone into the conversation.

GAMES. If you plan to play games, assemble your props and prizes ahead of time and keep them together in a convenient location. If you are going to play bridge, canasta, or poker, you usually mention the game in your invitation.

If you have planned on parlor games such as Charades, now fondly called "The Game," take it for granted that everyone is interested and wants to play. When you are ready, start right in explaining the rules. You're lost if you say brightly, "Now who wants to play games?" Everyone will probably groan, but once the game gets under way, the majority of people love it—particularly the ones who have groaned the loudest. Your own enthusiasm will usually influence the others, and soon there will be laughter and shouting.

TELEVISION. I believe that television will become more and more popular as a means of entertaining guests after dinner. It is a boon to the inexperienced hostess as it relieves her of the responsibility of keeping things going. However you should choose an outstanding program such as a "Spectacular," one that has a universal appeal. If you intend to watch a show of this kind, specify it in your invitation.

I don't think it is a good idea to turn on television in the middle of a party unless everyone attending is anxious to see a particular program.

MUSIC. Everyone loves to sing. If you have an obliging pianist, accordionist, or guitarist in your group, by all means plan some "barber shop" harmonizing as part of your entertainment.

PARTING IS SUCH SWEET SORROW

All good things must come to an end.

When guests say they must be leaving, don't try to force them to stay. Say that you are so happy that they could come, and how much they added to the party. Shake hands graciously and with affection, so that they leave with the happy certainty that you thoroughly enjoyed their company.

on being a Good guest

YOUR HOSTESS WILL LOVE YOU IF . . .

—you reply promptly to a written invitation whether it says RSVP or not.

—you accept a telephoned invitation with enthusiasm. If you wish first to check with spouse, call back as soon as possible.

—you don't let anything else interfere once you've accepted an invitation, except of course illness or other crisis.

—you dress up in your party best and enter gaily, as if you just know the party is going to be wonderful (not as if all assembled were lucky to have you there). If the hostess has not specified how guests are to dress, don't hesitate to call and ask her. It is embarrassing to find yourself overdressed or not dressed up enough.

—you arrive on time, neither too early nor more than fifteen minutes late. If you are unavoidably detained and will be more than thirty minutes late, call her to explain.

—you take some responsibility in introducing a newcomer to others at a large party. (The host or hostess will introduce him to one group. When that group breaks up, take the time to introduce him to another group before moving on yourself.) It is in perfectly good taste at a party to introduce yourself to anyone you don't know.

—you don't go overboard on the cocktails or other alcoholic beverages. One person who has overindulged can make everyone else uncomfortable.

On the other hand, if you don't care for alcoholic beverages, indicate to your host that you'd prefer a soft drink. The thoughtful host will always have one or two substitutes on hand.

—you eat heartily of the food which has been prepared for you, unless it is something which is injurious to your health. When a hostess plans, prepares, and serves good food, the guest who refuses it "because it has too many calories" is thoughtless indeed. Better to cut down the next day, or decline the invitation.

—you tell your hostess how much you are enjoying yourself. Don't keep it a secret. It will particularly help the inexperienced hostess overcome her qualms about the party, and give her courage to try again. Call her again the next day to thank her for including you, and tell her again how wonderful the party was. Mention the things you liked best about it.

—you are enthusiastic and entertaining. You have, in accepting the invitation, also accepted a responsibility to your hostess to help make the party a success. Don't plunk yourself down in one corner and remain there all evening. Don't huddle together with other members of your own sex. Women are always complaining of this, and yet they are the worst offenders. Move from group to group with the object of chatting with each other guest at some time during the evening, for that's what makes a party. It is fine to sit down for a cozy chat, but don't prolong it.

—you are pleasant to everyone, even though you are not too fond of someone there. Don't spoil the party by being rude or sulking, which may distress your hostess and other guests.

—you make a special point of chatting with the guest of honor if any, with out-of-town guests, with elderly people, or with shy guests. Instead of being self-conscious, and wondering "What do they think of me?" help draw other guests out and put them at ease. In particular, if you are the boss being entertained by a junior member of the firm, you should make a special effort to be gracious, amusing, and appreciative.

—you uphold your share of the conversation without monopolizing it. Always let another guest finish a story uninterrupted. If you have something to add to it, wait until he is finished.

—you avoid bringing distressing news to a party. Your hostess won't thank you for introducing a somber note to the festivities. Subjects to be avoided are:

Religion	Your ailments
Your maid troubles	Racial prejudices
Family troubles	Morbid items

—you offer to help, but don't insist on it. Many of us coordinate better alone.

—you enter whole-heartedly into games, contests, a sing-song, or whatever entertainment has been planned for you. Your enthusiastic support will give your hostess self-confidence.

—you refrain from setting glasses or burning cigarettes on furniture.

—you shake hands and say good-bye to the guest of honor and other guests as well as to the host and hostess.

—you don't keep host and hostess shivering in the doorway over lengthy good-byes.

One word more. . . . A good guest repays his or her social obligations. A single man or woman has just as much responsibility to do this as a married couple. It is not necessary to reciprocate on a lavish scale, but to return the kindness in some small way is a *must*.

Menu planning

SOME HELPFUL STEPS

1. Make a list of your favorite foods, particularly the ones you prepare well and easily. List under APPETIZERS, SOUPS, SALADS, MAIN DISHES, DESSERTS. Then when you start planning a special meal you can scan quickly through the list to get ideas. I keep my list in my recipe file. Choose main dishes first; they will guide you in your selection of other courses.

2. Experiment with recipes that sound good to you when you run across them in magazines, cook books, or newspapers. Even if you add only one new recipe a week to your repertoire, you'll soon become a very versatile cook. Here's a short cut: cut recipe from magazine or paper and staple it to a 3-by-5-inch card. Don't file it until you've tried it.

3. Shop carefully. Food must be of excellent quality for your recipes to turn out well.

4. Consider cooking time. If you are planning an oven dinner, try to choose dishes which will all require about the same amount of time.

5. Increase your knowledge of cooking by learning what vegetables "go" with what meat, such as sweet potatoes with baked ham. Experiment with different kinds of salads and dressings. Learn which ones complement which main courses, such as molded cranberry salad with turkey; cole slaw with fish; and tossed green salad with casserole dishes. Use relishes and sauces which go well with certain meats, such as mint sauce with lamb, applesauce with pork, and tartar sauce with fish.

6. Learn to use herbs and spices to trans-form your food from the everyday variety to something special, but don't get carried away. Too much seasoning can completely spoil a dish, and a little goes a long way. It is best to add your herbs in the last few moments of cooking.

7. Do not use one food in two ways in the same meal, such as corn on the cob and corn muffins, or tomato soup with tomato aspic.

8. Dramatize your food by using attractive garnishes—parsley, mint, or cherries. A spot of bright color makes an enormous difference.

CONTRAST

A study in contrast is necessary in planning palatable menus. The courses of a meal should combine opposite kinds of foods: the bland and the high flavored; fluid and solid; tart and sweet; hot and cold; starches and proteins. In addition to all this, contrasting color must be studied.

Bland and high-flavored food. Do not serve more than one strong-flavored food such as onions, cabbage, shrimp, or sardines, at one time.

Fluid and solid foods. Avoid serving foods which are all soft, such as soup, creamed chicken, and squash. Also avoid serving food which is all prepared the same way, such as creamed chicken with creamed peas.

On the other hand it is a mistake to serve food which is all solid, such as broiled steak, corn on the cob, and plum pudding.

Tart and sweet foods. Combine tart and sweet foods. If the meal tends to be on the sweet side, such as baked ham and pineapple, with sweet potatoes, etc., it would be well to serve a tart dessert such as lemon sherbet.

Hot and cold foods. It is usual and pleasing to the palate to have hot foods in the wintertime and cold foods in the summertime; however, a hot soup as an accompaniment to a cold meal is a welcome change, just as sherbet is a nice contrast with a hot meal.

Starches and proteins. Do not plan meals top-heavy in starches, such as potatoes, bread, and cornstarch pudding. Almost as bad is the meal composed entirely of proteins, such as meat, cheese, and eggs.

Contrasting colors. Do consider color. A menu consisting of creamed tuna, mashed potatoes, and cauliflower, will not have the eye appeal of a creamed dish, buttered beets, and broccoli. Avoid foods which clash in color, such as tomato sauce and beets.

Hostesses who specialize in table settings often plan menus which will complement their china, such as a pink dessert on pale green glass plates.

SUGGESTIONS ON PARTY MENUS

1. Plan a meal that can be prepared in advance, particularly if you have no help. Or plan food which can be prepared in front of your guests, such as steak broiled on barbecue or in the fireplace, shishkebabs, Sukiyaki dinner, or chafing dish specialties. Nowadays the electric skillet, roaster, deep-fat fryer, toaster, and griddle should all be put to work to make cooking more fun, and to leave you free to enjoy your guests. You might assign the broiling of the steaks to your husband or a friend, or call for a volunteer. You'll find that everyone likes to get in the act thus leaving you free to attend to last-minute preparations.

2. Do not plan too elaborate a meal. A plentiful supply of two or three dishes, deliciously cooked, pleases everyone. For instance, a most satisfying meal is one composed of a good hearty soup such as clam chowder (preferably served in a tureen), a salad, a crusty bread of some kind, dessert, and coffee.

3. Don't experiment with new dishes for a party. If you prepare meals you are sure of, you will have more confidence.

4. Don't serve too rich a meal; consider total calories. Your friends will be less than charmed if they have to diet for two days to offset your dinner.

5. Your guests will be happy with you if you avoid foods which are hard to digest, such as pork chops or mince pie.

6. If you decide to serve food such as lobster, shrimp, oysters, or Roquefort cheese, either make sure ahead of time that your guests like them, or prepare an alternate dish in case they don't like or can't eat your main dish.

7. For a buffet, plan foods which can be eaten with a fork alone.

8. Plan menus that will allow you to put your chafing dish to work. Not only does it add an exciting decorative note to your table, but it is practical for keeping food hot over a long period of time.

Your table

In order to entertain with a flair, it is necessary to have adequate equipment.

At one time, a white damask cloth, a china dinner set, and handsome silver were suitable for all kinds of entertaining. Today, however, with informality and self-service the vogue, we need a choice of table settings appropriate to various occasions. This does not necessarily mean different china for each one, but a variety of colorful cloths and accessories to make the over-all effect different.

In fact it is almost as important to have a variety of table settings as to have a variety of costumes in your wardrobe. You couldn't go to a ball in a sweater and skirt. Neither should you serve a semiformal dinner on a rough-textured cloth and pottery. You couldn't wear an evening gown to a barbecue. It is as incongruous to serve grilled hamburgers on a lace cloth and bone china.

ENCHANTING TABLE SETTINGS

Assembling attractive table settings can be a fascinating, creative and rewarding adventure, and it need not be expensive. Some of the most striking arrangements I've ever seen have cost less than $20 for the entire setting.

This included cloth or mats, napkins, silver-ware, china, glassware, centerpiece, candles, salt-and-pepper sets, and ashtrays.

It can't be done in a day. You have to shop carefully, watching for sales, noting new equipment as it comes out, visiting second-hand stores and antique shops—for you never know when you may run across that perfect finishing touch for a particular table. Watch for attractive accessories which will match or blend with what you already have—such as unusual candlesticks or flower containers. They will pay for themselves quickly as you need fewer flowers in your centerpiece if you use ornaments such as ceramic birds or china figures as part of it. Try for distinctive rather than costly ap-pointments. Color plays an important part; unusual color combinations together with out-of-the-ordinary decorations, service dishes, wicker baskets, and cook-at-the-table equip-ment contribute to making interesting tables.

True, there will be a certain amount of labor involved, apart from shopping for the various items. For instance, many times in order to achieve a certain unusual color scheme, you may have to make a tablecloth from yard goods. This you can usually do in as little as 45 minutes. The yard goods de-partment will give you some of your best inspiration for unusual table settings. Your cloth is of extreme importance, as it provides the background and frame for the whole arrangement. There is some labor involved in spraying that birdcage you picked up for 50 cents at the thrift shop. But think how pretty a pink birdcage will look filled with spring flowers at your May luncheon!

Even more important than the things you buy is the fact that, as you become more and more interested in this hobby and become more adept at visualizing how the finished product will look, you will develop new ideas for using things you already have. (For years I had a beautiful 15-inch-high Japanese figure of Italian porcelain sitting on a shelf.

One day I decided to use it as part of a floral centerpiece. The effect was breathtaking, and lifted that table from the ordinary to the exquisite.) Unfortunately the wedding gifts you receive are usually unrelated in both color and style. By accumulating several table settings of various degrees of formality, you may find a use for each of them.

You'll find that any effort, work, or time you put into this project will be repaid a thousand times by the admiration of your delighted family and friends.

Having exciting and novel table decora-tions makes you *want* to give parties. It adds to your confidence, and turns the ordinarily dull task of setting a table into a joy as you see beauty unfolding before your eyes.

Give some thought then to assembling two or three different table settings so that you will be equipped to plan not only semi-formal or company affairs, but informal parties, such as barbecues, and cook-at-the-table affairs.

The subject of table setting is a study in itself, and there are wonderfully interesting and informative books that I know you'll find very helpful. Here are a few of my favorites:

Roberts, Patricia Easterbrook, *The Book of Table Arrangements,* Crown Publishers, Inc., New York, 1951

Sprackling, Helen, *Setting Your Table,* M. Barrows & Company, Inc., New York, 1941, 1951

Hill, Amelia Leavitt, *The Complete Book of Table Setting,* The Greystone Press, New York, 1949

Lounsbery, Elizabeth, *Let's Set the Table,* Grosset and Dunlap, Inc., New York, 1938

Biddle, Dorothy, and Blom, Dorothea, *Table Setting for Everyone,* M. Barrows & Company, Inc., New York, 1949, 1951

Bailey, N. Beth, *Meal Planning and Table Service,* Manual Arts Press, Peoria, Illi-nois, 1924

GENERAL SUGGESTIONS

Be very careful to buy china, glassware, and silver in open patterns, so you can add more place settings or make replacements in case of loss or breakage. Buy from a store that has handled the pattern for some time and is likely to continue to do so.

In the long run you'll find it economical to buy a set of bone china. True, the initial expense is considerable, but in 20 years you may use up five sets of pottery through chipping and breaking. A bone china set will probably still be intact, and you will always derive so much pleasure from its beauty! Bone china is extremely strong, since bone is one of its materials; it will not chip and, despite its fragile appearance, needs no pampering. I have seen a salesman hold a dinner plate above his head and let it fall to the floor to prove that it will not break.

Don't overcrowd your table. Keep it in balance. A large bouquet at one end of the table would have to be balanced by tall candelabra or figurines at the other.

Using the same design in more than one appointment is attractive. If your silver pattern has a rose in its design, then china with roses on it would be a pretty addition. You may have a damask cloth with a lily design; if so, a bouquet of lilies as a centerpiece would be most appropriate.

Dress up your table for family meals as well as for parties. One small decoration, such as a tiny flag at each place on a patriotic holiday or a heart-shaped cake on Valentine's Day, transforms the simplest meal into a party.

HARMONY

To extend the comparison between a table setting and a costume, it isn't so much the value or beauty of any one part of the costume that is important as it is the harmony of the whole costume when seen together. No matter how pretty or unusual one item is, it will not appear to advantage unless it is wed with other things that complement it. For instance, a wicker bread basket would look out of place on a dainty organdy cloth, yet it looks perfect on a red-checkered one; in other words, you must consider not only the cloth and china, but the accessories as well. Even containers for your centerpiece should harmonize with the rest of the setting; for example, you might use silver or fine glass for a formal table, and pottery or copper for a casual one. And keep it in mind too, that a centerpiece for a tea or buffet may be high and full, whereas one for a seated dinner should be long and low so that guests can see one another across the table.

You may find yourself building a table setting around one outstanding accessory. You may have fallen heir to a magnificent silver épergne which you know you will be using at all your formal affairs. Naturally you will choose table appointments which will be formal enough to complement this lovely possession.

Brides, if possible, decide on colors and period of your dining room before making your selection of your tableware. Ornate china and delicate linen would be less attractive in a modern dining room than would contemporary patterns. Your table settings should harmonize with your dining room in color as well as period. If you are decorating your dining room in Chinese Modern with such strong colors as turquoise, red, and black, you will have to avoid pastel colors on your table.

APPROPRIATENESS

One of the most important features of table settings is their appropriateness to the occasion. Many factors enter into this:

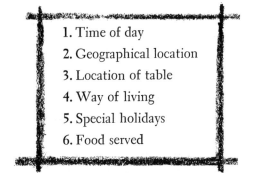

1. Time of day
2. Geographical location
3. Location of table
4. Way of living
5. Special holidays
6. Food served

1. Time of day. Breakfasts, lunches, and buffet suppers are usually much more informal than seated dinners. Appropriate for formal occasions are:

White damask or lace cloth

Bone china or other delicate chinaware

Stemmed crystal goblets and wines

Crystal, silver, or porcelain flower container

Fine flowers, such as roses, carnations, lilies, or bouvardia

Candelabra or candlesticks in silver, glassware, or porcelain

Appropriate for informal occasions:

Cloths of rough-textured materials or colored linen, cotton, or other fabrics, or place mats

Pottery or earthenware in solid colors or patterns

Heavy glassware, tumbler type

Flower containers in pottery, copper, or colored glass

Flowers such as zinnias, petunias, geraniums, or marigolds

Candlesticks of pottery, copper, brass, or wood

2. Geographical location. If you live in the southwestern United States, you may borrow Indian designs for your entertaining motif. If you live at an ocean resort, such as Cape Cod, you will probably prefer the nautical designs. In Honolulu you may set your table with a tropical air and strong oriental tendencies.

3. Location of table. If you're planning a table setting for a terrace or a picnic in the woods, you should plan a much more informal setting than you would for use in the dining room.

4. Way of living. If you are in the diplomatic corps or are on duty with one of the armed services on foreign soil, you will probably be expected to give many official functions, so you may want to entertain rather formally. On the other hand, if you live on a ranch, even though you may do as much entertaining, it might be on a more informal basis, and you would set your table accordingly.

5. Special holidays. Such holidays as Christmas, Halloween, and Easter give us wonderful opportunities to let imagination run riot. Even though there are traditional colors and symbols, there are countless ways we can improvise to achieve new effects. Don't neglect the old ones though. Who ever heard of Halloween without Jack-o-lanterns, witches, and black cats?

6. Food served. Here again use your imagination to achieve unusual effects. If you intend to serve Chinese food, why not give a little thought to a Chinese motif for your table, even if it's only a Chinese lantern and chopsticks.

COLOR

Bear in mind that your table covering is the background of your table setting. It provides the frame, so it is one of the most important items to consider.

Don't limit yourself to one cloth. If your china has a floral design made up of autumn colors, say brown, rust, yellow, and turquoise, any of these colors will make a striking background for it. This is a good thing to keep in mind when choosing your pattern. Your table appointments will assume different moods when used with different colors. Red is traditionally warm and festive, and is most used in the wintertime. Rust, brown, and orange are used in the autumn, while pink, lilac, yellow, and other pastels are lovely in the springtime. Blue, green, and white give a cool effect in the summertime.

CONTRASTS

These qualities make up an effective table setting:

> Contrast in colors
> Contrast in shapes
> Contrast in materials
> Contrast in heights

Contrast in colors. Combining table accessories could be compared to assembling different parts of a costume, or furnishing a room. There are certain basic rules which we follow. The first is contrast of color. If you have a rug or carpeting in a floral print, you would not use flowered draperies or slipcovers. You need the contrast of print and plain colors. So in your table settings, if you have a floral china pattern, use a solid color for your cloth or mats. If you use a flowered or print cloth, you must use perfectly plain china. (You see, I've made all of these mistakes myself—that is why I'm warning you. I have two beautiful cloths that are a joy to behold. One has a violet pattern, the other American Beauty roses and dark green leaves. I couldn't resist buying them. But alas, the only possible china one could use would be either plain white or green glass, neither of which I have. So there they lie still unused in the linen cupboard.)

That is why it is best to plan all your settings on paper before buying anything. You want to avoid winding up with a lot of odds and ends that just take up space in your cupboards.

Be careful in your use of color. Two contrasting colors are usually enough, although sometimes a touch of a third is effective. Mix-and-match chinaware can be very difficult to work with, because there are too many colors involved. One effective way it can be used is in setting up individual trays for a party. In this case, each tray can be done in a different color—one all-pink, one all-gray, etc.

You can also attain a striking effect by using color contrast in napkins; for example, you might use dark brown on a rust cloth.

If you use a dark cloth, choose light or floral dishes; avoid having all accessories dark or light.

Contrast in shapes. Try to avoid repeating the same shapes in your table arrangements; for instance, a round table, a round cloth, round dishes, and a round centerpiece would be monotonous. A better choice would be a round cloth, a rectangular centerpiece, and square dishes. Glasses with square bases make a good contrast to round tables.

Instead of buying dessert plates to match your china pattern, consider ones that will harmonize or contrast. For example, if you have round plates in a floral china pattern with a beautiful rose predominating, what could be prettier than square cranberry-colored glass dessert plates to use with it? Be sure though that the color matches the rose exactly.

Contrast in materials. The combination of china, glassware, and silver makes a table interesting and gives it distinction. Beware of using too much of any one material, such as silver serving dishes, silver goblets, silver butter dishes, and silver dinner plates. Can't you visualize how monotonous this would be, even though it would be a very rich table?

Contrast in heights. Instead of having all your appointments the same height, arrange some high spots and some low, such as a low centerpiece with very tall candles.

On a buffet or tea table, you can plan to use tall centerpieces and candelabra. This makes a good contrast to the other equipment which is necessarily low.

SETTING THE TABLE

No matter how carefully you have selected the different items for your table, the effect can be spoiled by careless placement. Take great care in setting your table neatly and in good taste, whether you are using your costliest appointments or paper materials.

Silence cloth: place it on the table so that it will hang evenly on all sides.

Cloth: place it over the silence cloth so that it will hang evenly with the crease straight down the center.

Place mats: space them evenly, with 20 to 24 inches between the center of each place setting and the one next to it.

Centerpiece: (so called no matter where it is placed) may be in the center, at one corner, or at one end of the table; always keep in mind that balance must be maintained.

Candles: set them at either end of centerpiece or at the four corners of it, forming a rectangle. If the centerpiece is placed at one end of the table, candles might be placed at the other to balance the arrangement.

Dinner or service plates: place them exactly in the center of the place mat 1 inch from the edge of the table; if you use a cloth, plates should be evenly spaced at an equal distance from one another.

Flat silver: place it 1 inch from the edge of the table. Forks are placed at the left of the plate, tines up, knives to the right with the cutting edge toward the plate. Spoons are placed to the right of the knives. Each piece of silver should be placed in order of use, beginning at the outside and working toward the plate.

Napkins: place on the service plate or to the left of the forks.

Butter plates: place above the forks with the butter knife laid across the plate—the cutting edge toward the user. Or, butter knives may be placed in a line with the rest of the silver.

Water goblets: place at the tip of the dinner knife. If a wine glass is used place it a little to the right and forward of the water glass.

Cigarette urns, ashtrays, matches: place between two place settings or above each plate.

Coffee service: place on side table with cups, saucers, teaspoons, and cream and sugar.

Place cards: place on the napkin on the plate, or above the plate.

Salt and pepper shakers: place between each two places. Individual pairs are above each plate.

Now in more detail:

SILENCE CLOTH

The use of a silence cloth makes for quieter service, gives a more luxurious look to the way the cloth lies, and protects the finish of the table. It should extend over the edges of the table about 5 inches, and if possible should be tied to the four corners to prevent slipping.

TABLECLOTH

1. Use a silence cloth underneath unless the cloth is of lace.

2. There should be approximately a 12- to 15-inch overhang on every side.

*3. Cloth must be immaculately pressed, with a single fold the length of the table.

4. Press an embroidered cloth on the wrong side first over a towel to bring out the design; then press it on the right side, ironing the crease in securely.

5. The line of the tablecloth should not be broken by chairs placed too close to the table.

PLACE MATS

1. These should be very carefully pressed, with no creases. A little starch makes them wonderfully crisp.

2. They should be spaced evenly on the table, with a distance of approximately 24 inches from the center of one mat to the center of the next one.

3. Do not use the center runner (which usually comes with a place mat set) if it overlaps the place mats. Many modern tables are too narrow to accommodate it gracefully.

---

* I find that pressing is easier if you place your ironing board at the end of the table and spread the cloth on it as you iron. A steam iron works wonders in freshening up linen just before using.

CENTERPIECE

1. Table decorations, including flowers, fruit, or figurines, are called centerpieces whether they are placed in the exact center or elsewhere on the table.

2. If the centerpiece consists of only one piece, it usually goes in the center. Twin centerpieces may be placed end to end down the center of the table, one on either side of a single candelabrum, or at the ends of the table if you decide to omit place settings there.

3. Select flowers or fruit, or a combination of both, and your container to harmonize with the color scheme and other accessories.

4. The centerpiece should be long and narrow so that your guests can see over it. It should not be so large that your table looks cluttered, and above all should not cascade into the water goblets or butter plates.

5. It should be evenly balanced and attractive from each place.

6. If you do not particularly enjoy flower arranging, why not leave this chore to a florist? It will cost very little more, particularly if you have to buy your flowers anyway. Take your container, and be explicit about color scheme and theme if any.

CANDLES

1. Flickering candlelight gives a soft glow that can transform an ordinary dinner table into a thing of beauty. It is not only the way it looks, but the way it makes you feel—a magic feeling of gaiety and well-being.

2. Candlesticks come in a variety of materials: silver, glass, fine china, and wood. Use whichever is most appropriate with your other accessories.

3. White or cream-colored tapers are considered the most beautiful, but colored candles are in good taste and are most attractive with certain table settings, particularly for special holiday affairs such as Christmas, Fourth of July, or Halloween, when color is all-important.

4. In order to bring the candle flame above eye-level, it is best to use tall candlesticks and long tapers. It is sometimes effective to use varied heights.

5. On the dinner table, candles are usually placed on each side of the centerpiece in a row or at the four corners to form a rectangle. If you have a single candelabrum, reverse the process. Place it in the center, flanked by twin centerpieces.

6. You should have at least one candle per person, to give sufficient light. If you have additional light, such as a lamp, four candles would suffice.

7. According to tradition, candles are never used for daytime parties—at least never before the tea hour. However, there is an exception. Candles are permissible if the day is so dark that artificial lighting is needed. (I love them so much myself that I'd like to use them at breakfast time.)

8. One parting caution: if candles are placed on the table, they should be lighted.

DINNER OR SERVICE PLATES

1. Service plates are usually to be found on the formal dinner table. They are about 1 inch larger than dinner plates. They harmonize with, but need not match the rest of the dinner set. As a matter of fact, china for each course may be of a different pattern as long as each harmonizes with the others.

2. For informal occasions, the dinner plate is used instead, particularly if the host or hostess serves the food.

3. It is a good idea to place the dinner plates as you are setting your table in order to judge the amount of space they will require. After the table is set, they may be whisked away for warming.

4. If you are using a service plate with a design on it, place it facing the guest.

5. A service plate remains in place until you are ready to serve the meat course. No food is placed directly on it; the appetizer and the soup are in their own containers, and these containers are placed on the service plate.

6. A word of caution: if your china has been on the shelf unused for a long time, it may need to be washed in hot suds. It is advisable to check this one day before you plan to use it.

SILVER

1. The pieces of flat silver you use will be determined by your menu. Never put silver on the table unless it is to be used.

2. Place silver, polished to its highest lustre, to the left and right of the plate in a straight line.

3. The cocktail fork is placed to the right of the spoons.

If salad is to be served before the meat course, place the salad fork to the left of the dinner fork; otherwise it goes on the right side of the dinner fork.

Dessert silver for an informal meal is usually in place throughout the meal. For a formal dinner, it is brought in with the dessert.

Teaspoons are placed on the saucer to the right of the cup. (Cups and saucers are on tray on side table.)

When iced-tea spoons are needed for long iced beverages, they are placed at the extreme right of other spoons.

4. Serving forks and spoons are placed to the right of the person serving. When a carving set is used, the fork could go on the left and the knife on the right, leaving a space between for the roast.

NAPKINS

1. Napkins for a formal dinner should match the tablecloth. They should be immaculately pressed, but not starched. Starch makes them too slippery, so that they slide to the floor.

2. Napkins should be folded simply, not into elaborate shapes. Accepted are:

> Square
>
> Rectangle
>
> Triangle, if placed beside the plate
>
> Triangle with two corners turned under and point toward diner
>
> Large squares, with sides folded under to make a flattened roll

3. Whether you use a tablecloth or mats at dinner, the napkin should be "dinner size," approximately 20 to 24 inches square.

4. When napkins are folded square or in an oblong, the folded edge may be toward the plate or away from it, as long as all napkins at the table are folded alike.

5. Two novel napkins have been introduced. One, called a "lapkin," is very practical in that it lies on the lap with little danger of slipping. It comes in 10-by-17- or 12-by-22-inch sizes. The other, suitable for buffets, is designed with flaps to hold silver, and can be rolled up and tied. Thus you have both napkin and silver rolled into one convenient packet.

BUTTER PLATES AND KNIVES

1. Butter plates and knives are almost always used at breakfasts, luncheons and informal dinners, but seldom at formal dinners.

2. The butter knife may be placed across the top of the butter plate, across the center of the plate, or aligned with the other silver with the tip pointing to the center of the table.

3. Butter plates need not match the rest of the china, but they should harmonize; there are very attractive ones in silver, glass, or pewter.

4. The butter plate is removed before the dessert course is brought in.

WATER GOBLETS

1. They should be sparkling clean. If you haven't used them for a while, check them the day before the party, and if necessary, wash in hot suds. A few drops of ammonia in the suds will make them really sparkle.

2. Goblets remain on the table throughout the meal.

3. When handling glasses with stems, hold them by the stem rather than the top.

4. Never use glasses that are nicked. Very small nicks can be smoothed with an emery board.

5. When serving iced tea or coffee or a fruit drink, place the glass on a small plate or saucer.

WINE GLASSES

If wine is served, the wine glass goes to the right of the water glass and a little bit forward.

PLACE CARDS

1. Place cards are a great convenience to the hostess when seating eight or more.

2. Not only does the use of place cards avoid confusion, it also gives the hostess the opportunity to seat guests she thinks will be especially congenial together.

3. Use white or ivory cards about the size of a visiting card. Some have silver or gold beveled edges, while others have the monogram or coat of arms of the hostess.

4. For a formal dinner, write Miss Jones or Mrs. Smith; for informal affairs where everyone knows each other, simply write John, Mary, or Aunt Alice. Use blue or black ink.

5. Place the cards either on the napkin on top of the service plate or in the space above the service plate.

6. Decorated place cards are sometimes used for special parties such as birthdays, Valentine's Day, etc.

SALT AND PEPPER SHAKERS

1. There should either be a pair between each two places or an individual pair above each place setting.

2. There is a wide choice of materials, including silver, china, and glass. Use whichever ones best harmonize with your other accessories.

3. Small open saltcellars are often seen on the formal table. With them use a tiny silver or mother-of-pearl spoon.

4. If your saltcellars have silver tops, it is a good idea to empty and wash them before storing to prevent corrosion.

CIGARETTE URNS, TRAYS, AND MATCHES

1. Small cigarette containers, usually of silver or crystal, small ashtrays, and matches or lighters should be between each two place settings or above each place setting. (Place cards can be propped up against the tray.)

2. Smoking material is almost always used on the breakfast, luncheon, or informal dinner table, and sometimes on the formal table. Some hostesses prefer to have cigarettes passed after the dessert course.

3. If you place smoking equipment on the table, it will be assumed that you do not object to smoking throughout the meal.

4. Do not place packages of cigarettes on the table.

5. If you do not have small matched cigarette containers, place two cigarettes across a small ashtray, with a tiny box of matches. (Little Swedish matches are dainty on the table and monogramed or personalized matchbooks would also be suitable.)

CUPS AND SAUCERS

1. Although cups and saucers are usually placed on a tray on a side table, then brought to the table at dessert time for the hostess, many people prefer coffee with meals, and the hostess may prefer having the coffee service in front of her throughout the meal. This is particularly true at breakfast time.

2. Coffee for an informal dinner is served either at the table or in the living room. Coffee for a formal dinner is almost always served in the living room, usually in small, after-dinner cups with small, after-dinner coffee spoons.

These need not match your other china or silver.

3. When assembling cups and saucers on a tray, arrange all cup handles to the right in approximately the same position, with the teaspoon on the saucer at the right.

(Although the preceding suggestions on table setting apply primarily to the semiformal dinner, I believe you will be able to use them as a guide for all of your table setting. Even though you will use a great variety of materials, from bone china to paper plates, the general rules are the same.

HOW TO INCREASE TABLE SPACE

A few of the devices that, for large parties, can be used to increase table space are:

- A piece of heavy plywood set over a smaller surface.
- A piece of plywood set on two or three saw horses.
- Two or three card tables placed together, then covered with a single cloth.
- A round Extenda-top table which fits over a card table and increases the seating capacity to six. (These fold in the center for easy storage.)

- Aluminum portable tables; they come in various sizes, and will seat six to ten people depending on the size.
- An 18-inch shelf running the length of your dining room is convenient for buffet suppers. Paint the shelf to match the other woodwork.
- Maybe you have an extra door stored in your basement. If it is solid and without decoration, it will make a fine low table if it is placed over matching coffee tables, then covered with a cloth. (This would be particularly suitable for either the Chinese or Japanese parties.)

Methods of serving

For an informal party, here are a few suggestions for serving buffet meals without a maid:

Guests serve themselves from a buffet set on the dining-room table, then return to the living room to eat. If possible there should be a snack table between each two guests. In serving this way, remember to plan food that can be handled with the fork alone.

Guests serve themselves from a buffet, serving table, or serving shelf, then sit at the dining-room table which has been set as if for a conventional dinner.

Food is set on the dining table. Guests serve themselves, then eat at card tables or round Extenda-top tables which have been fully set in advance.

Guests serve themselves from the dining-room table on which is not only food, but napkins and silverware as well. Guests sit at card tables which have only a cloth on them. This method is especially suitable if you have a small house or apartment, as the tables can be set up at the last minute.

SUGGESTIONS FOR USING
SERVING TRAYS

Trays are very practical and are being designed in a variety of attractive shapes and colors. Adequate serving trays can be purchased for as little as 50 cents each. Three methods of using trays in serving are:

1. Trays are set in advance and placed on a large surface, such as an extended dining-room table. Filled plates, salads, and rolls are set on the tray. Each guest picks up one and carries it back to the living room.

2. Trays are stacked at one end of the table cafeteria-style. The host carves and serves the meat and the hostess serves the vegetables and salad and puts a roll on the guest's plate. He then picks up his napkin and silverware and carries the tray to the living room.

3. Snack table service is much like the first method described, except that standing trays are used. Filled plates, salad, and rolls are set on the tray, which is then brought in by the host and placed near each guest.

DESSERT

Dessert may be either served by the hostess or placed in a convenient location where the guests may feel free to serve themselves.

COFFEE

Coffee may be served from a tray in front of the hostess or brought in from the kitchen already poured. If she wishes, the hostess can pass a tray on which are three or four filled cups, sugar, and cream. Guests help themselves to sugar and cream from the tray as it is passed.

Another method is to place the coffee service in a central location at the beginning of the meal so that guests may have coffee at any time they wish.

DESSERT AND COFFEE
ON TEA WAGON

Tea wagons are becoming very popular again and are tremendously useful in serving at parties. The wagon can be wheeled in after guests have finished the main course. Dessert and coffee are on the top shelf. Each guest places his plate on the lower shelf as the cart reaches him; he is then served dessert and coffee, and the cart goes on to the next guest. In this way coffee and dessert can be served in a minute or two.

HOST AND HOSTESS
TAKE TURNS SERVING

When entertaining remember that either the host or hostess should be with guests at all times; a little teamwork is required to make things go smoothly. Some young friends of ours have worked out this easy routine:

Margaret sets food on the table and calls guests to dinner.

Guests serve themselves and return to the living room.

John sets up small tables near the guests.

After the main course Margaret requests her guests to return to the dining room and serve themselves coffee. During this interval she removes dishes.

After she returns, John brings in desserts on a tray and passes them.

Margaret removes dessert dishes while John serves liqueurs.

(If host is reluctant to help in this way, I'm sure a close friend would give you a hand. However, don't let guests help with the dishes. Nothing breaks up the party atmosphere so quickly.)

TWO CHARTS OF BUFFET ·TABLES

If you need extra space, push your table against the wall and arrange the centerpiece and candles toward the back of the table. It might look something like this:

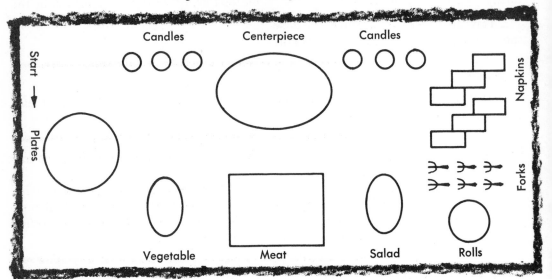

If you have a large number of guests, set the table in the center of the room, and duplicate the service on each side of table to expedite things:

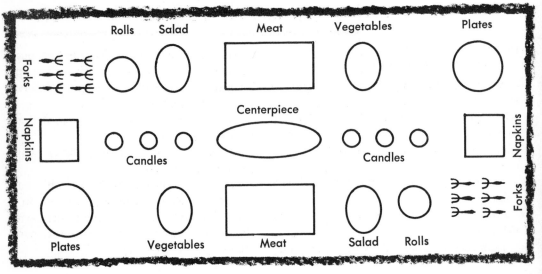

3 WAYS OF SERVING WITHOUT A MAID

1. Salad or soup is at each place when dinner is announced.

When the first course is finished, the hostess removes plates to the kitchen.

She serves plates in the kitchen, carries them into the dining room, and sets them before the guests.

When the main course is finished, the hostess removes plates to the kitchen.

She then brings in dessert on individual plates.

Coffee is served in the living room.

2. Family-style serving is still popular in many parts of the country. A dinner plate is placed in front of each person. Food is set on the table in platters and vegetable bowls and passed along from one diner to the next.

3. English service. A soup or salad is in place when guests are called to dinner.

The hostess removes plates when the first course is finished; she then brings in the main course, possibly on a teacart. (Hot plates, the roast, vegetables, and rolls.)

The host has a stack of plates in front of him. He carves and serves the meat course and passes each plate to his left. The hostess serves the vegetables and passes the plate to her left, so that the guest to the right of host gets the first plate.

Rolls are passed in a basket.

At the conclusion of the main course, possibly with the help of one guest, the hostess removes the meat platter, vegetable dishes, rolls, salts and peppers, and used dishes. Here again the teacart will be useful.

She then brings in the dessert, which she serves at the table.

Coffee is served in the living room.

This could be done smoothly for six or eight persons. The most important thing to remember is not to hurry. Guests do not mind; in fact, are seldom aware of the lapse of time between courses; even in restaurants this is expected. Guests are more interested in the conversation than in your serving of the dinner.

PARTY MAID

Few of us have full time help these days; however we may be able to get part time help for a party. I believe you'll find it much safer to have a personal interview with a prospective party maid or cateress than to determine by telephone whether or not she will be satisfactory. A pleasant, well-mannered, reliable maid of good appearance can help make a party successful. She can raise the spirits of the hostess by giving her confidence that everything is going to go smoothly; an undesirable maid can have the opposite effect. Personally, I would far rather do without a maid than have one with a surly disposition.

By asking the prospective maid how she serves, you will be able to find out if she is experienced, and whether or not her method of doing things is the one you prefer. At the same time, you will be giving her an opportunity to find out whether she would like to work for you, and whether her experience is adequate for your needs.

It is important to remember that unless you yourself know the mechanics of serving a seated meal or buffet, you can't reasonably expect to receive perfect service from others.

If you are planning a seated dinner, it would be wise to have a rehearsal to ensure smooth serving during the party. Try to keep your serving informal and uncomplicated, particularly the first time or two that you engage your party maid. After she has become acquainted with you, your kitchen, and the way you like things served, she will probably be willing to try more elaborate service.

When the maid leaves, thank her for helping you. If she has done a good job, tell her so.

Have the correct change ready to pay her.

PRELIMINARY ARRANGEMENTS

When making preliminary arrangements, these points should be understood clearly by both parties:

Salary. Wages vary in different sections of the country; some cateresses charge by the day or evening, but the majority charge by the hour. Many set a minimum for their services. Find out whether you are expected to pay carfare.

Hours. Specify the exact hour you expect your maid, and estimate as closely as possible how long her services will be needed.

Duties. Advise the maid approximately how much cooking and serving will be involved, and whether or not she will be expected to answer the door. (It is not advisable for the maid to answer the door if she is doing the cooking.)

Uniform. Find out if she has her own uniform, and if it is one of which you approve.

Transportation. Find out whether the maid will provide her own or expect you to take her home or to the bus stop. Give her clear directions to your home.

❲ *It is much better to have a mutual understanding of all of these things in advance than to have things go wrong at the last minute.*

STEP BY STEP

There are many different types of parties, and the serving for each can be unique. It might be helpful to describe one party from the time the party maid arrived.

Since Mrs. Brown was engaging Sally for the first time, Sally came an hour early.

First, Sally was shown where to hang her coat and hat, and where she could freshen up and change into her uniform.

Mrs. Brown then showed the maid the kitchen. She pointed out where the pots and pans were kept, where the dish towels were, where she kept the soap and cleansers, etc. As a double-check she called Sally's attention to a typewritten list tacked up over the sink to which she could refer in case she forgot where anything was.

This is an excellent idea when you have to rely on part-time help. Many times you can't get the same party maid, and this list will save much time and prevent confusion:

Dish towels.........Second drawer
Pots and pans.......Bottom shelf in pantry
Soap and cleansers...Cupboard under sink

She next showed Sally the dining room. The table was set for a buffet. Mrs. Brown had the serving platters, vegetable dishes, salad bowl, and roll basket all in place on the table with a slip of paper in each telling what food it was for. In this way Sally was able to set the food on the table when ready. Serving forks and spoons were near each serving dish.

They then returned to the kitchen where Mrs. Brown showed Sally the menu and instructions. This list was tacked up over the sink so that it could be referred to easily.

Buffet Supper for 12

(at 7:30)

Baked Ham   Creamy Mustard Sauce
(ready)

Candied Sweet Potatoes
(ready)

Green Peas with Sliced Mushrooms

Bleu Cheese Mousse on Salad Greens
(ready)

Home-made Rolls
(are rising, have to be baked)

Baba au rhum
(ready)

Coffee

PREPARATION OF FOOD

6:15 Pour glaze over ham. Do not remove twine.
Bake at 325 degrees 1 hour.

6:30 Bake sweet potatoes covered for 45 minutes at 325 degrees, uncovered an additional 15 minutes at 350.

6:45 Slice mushrooms, sauté in margarine, set aside.

7:00 Make the coffee. Keep hot over very low flame.

7:15 Remove ham from oven and keep in warm place.

7:20 Turn up heat to 350 degrees. Bake rolls 10 minutes or until brown on top. Place inside napkin in roll basket.
Arrange a bed of shredded salad greens on serving plate. Unmold bleu cheese mousse salads.
Set back in ice box. Place on table just before guests are called to dinner.

7:25 Cook peas until just tender in very small amount of water. Drain. Add butter and mushrooms. Place in covered, heated vegetable dish.

7:30 Place all food on the table. Place hot things on asbestos pads. Remove twine from ham. Place mustard sauce in sauceboat next to ham.

CHECK-OFF LIST

ham	peas
mustard sauce	salad
sweet potatoes	rolls

7:45 Whip the cream and sweeten a little with 1 tbsp. confectioner's sugar. Remove babas from refrigerator and place each on a dessert place. Top each with a blob of whipped cream.

SERVICE

Shortly before dinner is ready:

Fill pitcher with ice water and place on tray with glasses.

Cut and arrange butter pats on plate. Set on table.

As guests are serving themselves in the dining room, remove cocktail glasses and empty ashtrays from the living room.

Pass hot rolls as soon as guests need "seconds."

When guests are finished with main course, remove used plates to kitchen.

Set coffee tray in front of me on the coffee table in the living room. (Coffee, sugar, cream, spoons.)

Serve dessert to the guests.

Refill coffee pot. If necessary, make fresh coffee.

When you finish washing and drying the dishes, please set them in cupboards. I'll rearrange later if necessary.

Mrs. Brown excused herself from her guests at 7:15 to help Sally get dinner on the table. After she had helped Mrs. Brown two or three times, Sally was able to manage alone. Mrs. Brown told her to take time out to have her own dinner after serving.

part II
parties for all occasions

INTRODUCTION

In Part Two, we will combine the general suggestions for menus, table settings, games, and other details into a coordinated whole. The majority of these parties follow a theme throughout.

If you do not want to follow any one of these plans exactly, select the parts that appeal to you and eliminate the others. You will also want to adapt the parties to your own circumstances.

REGARDING THE SECTION ON TABLE SETTINGS. Naturally you are not going to buy new equipment to duplicate the table settings I've described, but they may give you some ideas that will help you to combine more effectively the china, table linen, and glassware you already have.

REGARDING RECIPES. In cases where I have found, for a particular recipe, that any one product is superior in flavor to the average, I have given the brand name. Almost all recipes are made up of ingredients which can be found in the average grocery store or supermarket.

REGARDING SERVICE. The majority of hostesses entertain today without help of a maid. The following parties were planned with this fact in mind.

REGARDING SCHEDULES. Detailed schedules have not been given for every party, but you will be able to work out your own easily by referring to the Party Plan, pages 7–10.

REGARDING INVITATIONS, FAVORS, ETC. The materials used in making invitations, favors, and other novelties can be found in most variety stores or mail-order catalogues.

REGARDING GROCERY LISTS. Because the number of guests will vary, no quantities are mentioned in most grocery lists, nor are staples, such as flour, sugar, coffee, spices, etc.

A morning coffee

This comparatively new type of party is rapidly becoming a very popular form of entertaining. Among its most endearing qualities is its informality in terms of both dress and methods of serving. Moreover, the food need not be elaborate, which makes it an inexpensive way of entertaining.

Of shorter duration than other parties, lasting usually from 10:30 to 11:30 or 12 o'clock, the Coffee allows guests time to arrive home before their school-age children, thus eliminating baby-sitter fees. In addition to these advantages, both hostess and guests are at their best in the morning—fresh and rested and eager for a chat.

A Coffee provides a pleasant way to introduce your mother, sister, or other house guest to your friends. It is also a gracious but simple way to welcome a new neighbor or say good-bye to an old one. A morning Coffee is also a hospitable way in which to start or conclude a committee meeting.

Instead of the more elaborate luncheon or tea to shower a bride or expectant mother, many hostesses prefer to give an informal morning Coffee. It is an especially practical idea during the summer months.

YOU ARE INVITED

Card companies are now putting out some very smart and amusing Coffee invitations. One I used recently had a picture of a grinning coffee pot on the cover saying HOW ABOUT A CUP OF COFFEE? Inside were spaces giving time, date, occasion, and other pertinent information. (I think many times clever invitations set a mood for a party. The invitation intimates that it's to be an informal "fun" party, and guests accordingly arrive with happy expectations.)

However, written invitations are not at all necessary, and telephoned ones have one great advantage, in that you know at once how many guests to expect, and can complete your plans promptly.

IT'S SUMMERTIME

If you are lucky enough to have a home of your own, you might invite your friends to sit out on the terrace or patio, on the lawn under the trees, or on a covered veranda, where it's cool and you can all relax.

A FLOWER-FRESH TABLE

Table. Here's an opportunity to use your picnic table, an umbrella table, or an aluminum folding table that opens up to 72 inches or more.

Cloth. A vivid cloth with white fringe looks particularly festive for outdoor entertaining. Keep in mind one of the basic rules of table setting. If your dishes have a design, use a cloth in a solid color; on the other hand, a gaily flowered cloth is pretty if your dishes are plain. Be careful to choose colors that harmonize.

Napkins. Napkins should either match or harmonize with the cloth, and may be of linen or paper. (A pretty effect can be obtained by using napkins in all the colors of the rainbow. For instance, on my dark brown cloth, I sometimes use napkins in yellow, coral, turquoise, green, pink, and blue. Most novelty and department stores have paper napkins in a variety of colors.)

China. Your pottery or earthenware will be perfect in this setting. I advise using cups only on dessert plates, for easier handling. There are now available "tea and toast" sets which are very practical. The cup fits into an indentation at one side of the plate, leaving the rest of the space free for sandwiches, toast, or cookies, as the case may be.

Centerpiece. Flowers to harmonize with your other colors can be such old-fashioned favorites as geraniums, marigolds, petunias, or zinnias. I love to see a casually arranged bouquet of seasonal garden flowers. Or, as a more unusual alternative, you might make an interesting and colorful centerpiece with well-scrubbed vegetables.

Serving dishes. Wicker containers (either flat ones such as a wicker leaf, or wicker baskets) are attractive and practical for an informal table. At one party I attended, the hostess had filled a wicker cornucopia with cookies iced in various colors and had tipped it so that the cookies spilled out onto the cloth. She used it as a centerpiece, thus eliminating the need for flowers.

HOW TO SERVE

Coffee can either be passed around on a tray, followed by the sweet rolls and cookies, or it can be set out on the table, with a friend pouring and guests helping themselves to their own tidbits from the table.

IT'S WINTERTIME

Choose the coziest spot in the house—den or play room—or make a circle in front of the living-room fireplace where you can all sit comfortably and chat. So that no one will have to miss anything by leaving the room, set up your serving table nearby.

Of course if it's a large affair, guests will be moving from one group and one room to another, so I'd suggest setting your dining table for informal buffet-type serving.

Ask a good friend to pour and, if you don't have a party maid, ask someone to help you replenish the serving dishes as needed.

A PRETTY TABLE

I see this as a slightly more formal affair than the summertime Coffee, so we shall decorate the table accordingly.

Cloth. To bring out the design and color scheme of your best china most effectively, choose a cloth in a solid color.

Napkins. Use either linen or paper napkins, either matching or harmonizing with the cloth.

China. If you are using pieces from a set of china, I'd advise you to use only cups and plates. If you prefer to use a collection of odd cups and saucers, it is not only acceptable, but adds a pleasing note. Moreover, tales of how, when, and where you collected them can sometimes make for very interesting conversation.

Centerpiece. Any of these would be appropriate: flowers in a crystal bowl; a handsome fruit arrangement on a silver platter; flowering house plants flanked by china ornaments.

Candles. As I mentioned earlier although candles are not as a rule considered appropriate for daytime use, there are exceptions: either if a dining room has no daylight, or if the day is so dark that artificial light is needed, candles may be substituted.

I'll never forget the Coffee a friend gave for Marine wives in Newport, Rhode Island.

It was a dark, snowy winter morning. As we entered, our beaming hostess greeted us affectionately, and we were met by a roaring wood fire, and flickering candles everywhere —the buffet, on the mantel, on tables. The effect was beautiful; all the guests loved it and had a most happy time.

Menu

*Pineapple Cubes and Strawberries
dipped in powdered sugar*

Marguerite Baker's Tiny Biscuits

Choice of Jams and Relishes

Toasted Marmalade Strips

Struzzel-filled Coffee Cake

Mrs. McCormick's Lace Cookies

Coffee

* Starred items will be found in the recipe section.

(In the summertime, it is a good idea to have a frosty fruit drink as well.

RECITES

PINEAPPLE CUBES AND STRAW-BERRIES, POWDERED SUGAR DIP

With sharp knife, cut straight down through pineapple, crown and all. Then cut again, making four sections. (Be sure to leave crown on. This is what makes the dish so pretty.)

With serrated knife, cut out the meaty section, leaving shell intact. Remove the pithy center. Cut the remainder into 1-inch cubes. Insert toothpick into each cube. Re-place cubes in pineapple shells. Arrange sections on a plate or platter with a bowl of confectioner's sugar for dunking purposes. Arrange strawberries, with hulls left on, alternately with the pineapple. When strawberries are out of season, I spear a small piece of maraschino cherry with each cube of pineapple to give color contrast.

MARGUERITE BAKER'S TINY BISCUITS

2¼ cups flour	4 tbsp. shortening
2½ tsp. baking powder	2 tbsp. butter
1¼ tsp. sugar	¾ cup milk
1¼ tsp. salt	

Mix and sift dry ingredients. Cut in the shortening. Add milk gradually, mixing to a soft dough. Toss on a floured board. Roll lightly to ¼-inch thickness. Cut out with very small biscuit cutter (1½ inches). Bake 20 minutes at 400 degrees. Arrange on plate circled by several small bowls of jams and jellies. Suggestions are Orange Cranberry Relish, Plum Conserve, Raspberry Jam, Honey Butter (equal proportions of softened butter and honey), and Pear Honey.

Marguerite is an excellent cateress famous for these biscuits throughout Navy circles in Newport, Rhode Island. She makes and half bakes them at home. Thought you'd like to know that you can prepare them in advance, then pop them into the oven for the last 10 minutes.

TOASTED MARMALADE STRIPS

1. Make orange marmalade sandwiches, omitting butter.

2. Cut off the crusts.

3. Fry slowly in margarine (like French toast) until brown.

4. Cut in three strips.

   Serve hot.

STRUZZEL-FILLED COFFEE CAKE

Sift together:	Cut in:
1½ cups flour	¼ cup shortening
3 tsp. baking pow- der	1 beaten egg
¼ tsp. salt	½ cup milk
¾ cup sugar	Mix well

Add 1 tsp. vanilla

Filling:

2 cups loosely packed brown sugar	4 tsp. cinnamon
4 tbsp. flour	4 tbsp. melted butter
	½ cup nuts

Pour half of mixture into greased Pyrex pie
plate. Cover this with half of the filling.
Add the rest of the batter.
Add the rest of the filling.
Bake 25 minutes at 375 degrees.
To serve, cut in small wedges. Add butter if
desired.
(Serve hot)

MRS. McCORMICK'S LACE COOKIES

1 cup brown sugar	¼ tsp. baking soda
1 cup rolled oats	1 tbsp. lemon juice
1 tbsp. flour	⅓ cup melted butter

Combine ingredients.
Drop by teaspoonfuls on ungreased cookie
sheet, about 3 inches apart.
Bake in 325-degree oven until brown. Remove from cookie sheet while still warm.

(*This makes a quite different dessert if it is made
into cornucopias while still warm and filled with
whipped cream or ice cream.*

Rock-a-bye baby shower

Sue's gaiety and excitement about a "forth-coming event" has put her friends in a festive mood too, and all feel that a party is in order.

The rivalry as to who should give her the shower is resolved when the girls decide to *all* get into the act.

PRELIMINARY GET-TOGETHER

Shirley has a large charming house, so it is to be held there; but apart from that, it is a no-hostess affair. It's delightfully easy this way, as all work and expenses are divided.

Two or three girls get together over coffee, plan the party, and assign jobs.

Two girls each for the following:

Food
Games and prizes
Table setting
Invitations and presentation of gifts
Mopping-up operations

Approximate schedule of events:

12:45 Guests arrive

1:30 Lunch

2:15 Games

3:00 Open shower gifts

ROCK-A-BYE BABY INVITATION

Cut piece of music manuscript paper 3¼ by 6¼ inches. Copy the music and words.

Cut gift wrapping paper (I used a soft yellow) or construction paper 7 by 13 inches. Fold top to bottom, then fold crosswise. Staple or paste the music to inside section; it will fit regulation-size envelopes.

On the cover, write or print particulars; for example:

ROCK-A-BYE BABY SHOWER FOR SUE

AT SHIRLEY CAMPBELL'S

45 SHADY LANE DRIVE

TO SAY WELCOME

Welcoming the guests as they arrive is Mr. Stork himself, attached to the front door. Suspended from his beak is a basket filled with flowers—possibly from your own garden.

Many baby specialty shops will loan storks for a shower. The one I have is made of plastic and is 12 inches high, but a larger one could be used.

For the living room, make a flower arrangement in a doll's cradle or baby buggy.

SELF-SERVICE PUNCH BAR

If the party is held in the summer, a bowl filled with well-iced fruit punch will be most welcome. Have a few berries or thin slices of pineapple floating around, and for extra glamour, tuck a sprig of mint coated with confectioner's sugar in each glass or punch cup. To get the party off to a good start, guests serve themselves as they arrive.

EVERYBODY HELPS

To assure hot food and a cool cook, pass a tray containing slips of paper with a job written on each.

List of tasks:

1. Please keep punch bowl refilled.
2. Please pass cigarettes and keep ashtrays emptied.

3. Please fill water glasses and put on butter at 1:30.
4. Please toss the salad at 1:30 and set on table.
5. Please keep hot-roll dish filled.
6. Please clear dishes from main course and later from dessert course and stack.

7. Please serve dessert.
8. Please pour coffee and keep replenished.
9. Ouch!!! Everything happens to you—kitchen clean-up duty.
10. This is *not* your lucky day. You help number 9.

A DAINTY TABLE

Card tables will be set, but guests will serve themselves from a buffet table.

Not knowing whether the baby will be in the "sugar and spice" or the "snips and snails" category, we have discarded the pink and blue color scheme and adopted a sunshine yellow for the buffet table. The table setting committee will buy 5 yards of dimity, white, with sprigs of yellow roses, and seam it down the center. This will make a cloth approximately 72 by 90 inches. They will also buy 1 yard each of pink, pale blue, and lilac for the card tables in the same pattern. These cloths can be made in no time on the sewing machine. They wash and iron like handkerchiefs and can be used for future parties. Sprigged dimity is available in most places in a variety of charming colors.

BABES IN THE WOOD

How to make Rock-a-bye Baby centerpiece

Small branches and twigs sprayed green are secured in sand in a white flowerpot. On the "tree" are hung miniature cradles made from eggshells, and tiny sprays of artificial flowers, such as the bouquets sold at the ten-cent store for boutonnieres.

Here's a close-up view
of the rock-a-bye baby

To make cradles

Use halves of eggshells which are fairly uniform around the top and do not have too many cracks. Remove the thin membrane and wash and dry the shell carefully. Paint the eggshells inside and out in pastel colors with poster paint. Let the shells dry and then fill each one about halfway with melted wax. When the wax is almost hardened, stick in tiny sprigs of artificial flowers and tuck a tiny rubber baby, swathed in tulle, in among the flowers. (These are adorable babies, measuring 1¼ inches and available at the ten-cent store for five cents each.) To complete the cradle, attach the ends of a pipe cleaner in the melted wax at each side to form the handle by which it is suspended from the tree. A bow of baby ribbon may be attached to the handle if desired. Some of the cradles may be filled with chenille baby chicks such as those used at Easter time. Each guest receives a cradle as a favor.

PLACE CARDS

From a printer or stationer, buy a 25-by-20 inch sheet of very thin, yellow cardboard and cut it into 4-by-2½-inch pieces. Fold top of each piece of cardboard to bottom, and from the center of the folded edge, cut out a half circle big enough to accommodate a tiny rubber baby. A little below the half circle, make two small holes for the baby's feet with scissors or hole puncher. Insert a small piece of net and the baby in the top hole and the baby's feet through the lower holes. Paste tiny blossoms on each side of the baby.

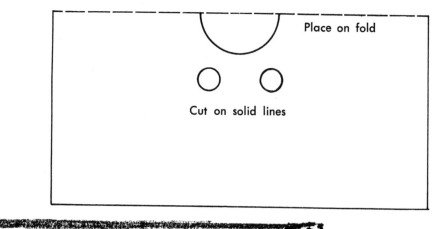

Place on fold

Cut on solid lines

Menu

Iced Fruit Punch
(served before lunch)

*Tuna Newburg in Noodle Ring

*Stuffed Tomatoes flanked by Lettuce Rolls

Brown 'n Serve Rolls

*Storks' Nests

Tea   Coffee

Candied walnuts for nibbling

* Starred items will be found in the recipe section.

RECIPES

BAKED NOODLE RING

1 8-oz. pkg. noodles
3 eggs
2¼ cups milk
½ cup cracker crumbs, rolled fine
¾ cup grated sharp cheese
¾ tsp. salt
¼ tsp. fresh ground pepper
2 tsp. Worcestershire sauce
½ cup finely chopped almonds
Lawry's Seasoned Salt

Cook the noodles 10 minutes in boiling salted water. Drain, then put them in collander. Rinse in cold water for a few minutes and drain well.

Beat the eggs, then add all the other ingredients. Pour into well-buttered ring mold. Place the mold in a pan of hot water. (The purpose of the hot water is to prevent the noodle ring from forming a crust around the inside of the mold while baking.)

Bake at 350 degrees about 40 minutes. Test it with a silver knife. When the knife comes out clean, it is done. While the noodle ring is baking, you can be preparing the Tuna Newburg filling as follows:

TUNA NEWBURG IN NOODLE RING

Serves 6

2 cups tuna	2 egg yolks beaten
4 tbsp. butter or	salt
margarine	pepper
4 tbsp. flour.	½ tsp. paprika
2 cups light cream	¼ cup sherry if desired

Melt butter in top of double boiler. Blend in flour. Add cream, stirring constantly. Pour part of cream mixture into beaten egg yolks and mix thoroughly. Then pour mixture back into the hot cream sauce. Stir until thickened. Add a little of the cream sauce to the sherry. Mix thoroughly, then pour mixture back into the cream sauce. Add tuna, then seasoning. When ready to serve, heat thoroughly in the double boiler and pour into baked noodle ring.

STUFFED TOMATOES FLANKED BY LETTUCE ROLLS

Select fairly large, ripe, firm tomatoes, one for each person. Scoop out centers. Fill with a mixture of hard-boiled eggs, chopped beets, chopped celery, and a little onion—all tossed carefully with home-made boiled dressing.

Lettuce rolls. Combine ¼ cup chopped sweet pickle, ½ tsp. chopped onion, 2 tbsp. mayonnaise with a pint of cottage cheese. Spread on lettuce leaf, roll, and fasten with toothpick. Serve 2 lettuce rolls with each stuffed tomato.

ALICE'S "STORKS' NESTS" DESSERT

A heavenly creation to eat as well as to look at!

4 egg whites	1 qt. strawberry ice
¼ tsp. cream of tartar	cream (to fill the
1 cup sugar	meringues)
½ tsp. vanilla	

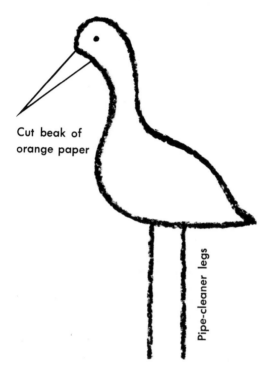

Cut beak of orange paper

Pipe-cleaner legs

Beat egg whites and cream of tartar until stiff and dry. Gradually add ⅔ cup of sugar. Continue beating until mixture holds shape. Add vanilla. Fold in the remaining ⅓ cup sugar. Drop from tablespoon onto greased baking sheet 1 inch apart. Bake in 275-degree oven about 30 minutes or until firm. Makes about 16 meringues. Fill with strawberry ice cream, and then you insert a small stork.

To make storks

1. Spread out a small roll of cotton flat on the table.
2. Carefully separate it until you have two layers.
3. Lay stork pattern on cotton. With small sharp scissors, cut around the pattern. This gives you the body of the stork.
4. Cut beak of orange construction paper. Insert between layers of cotton and secure with a drop of du Pont glue.
5. Insert pipe-cleaner legs between layers of cotton. Secure with du Pont glue if necessary.
6. A dot of India ink for each eye, and there you are. Pull or brush cotton gently for a fluffy effect.

⟨ *These take about five minutes each to make.*

As an alternative, bakeries usually carry plastic storks 3 or 4 inches high for 20 to 25 cents. These make attractive "take-home" items.

CANDIED WALNUTS

5 cups California	1½ tsp. salt
walnut halves	1½ tsp. cinnamon
3 cups orange juice	2 tsp. vanilla extract

Heat the walnuts in medium oven (375 degrees) about 15 minutes, stirring often. Cool the walnuts. Cook orange juice, cinnamon, and salt to soft ball stage (236 degrees) without stirring. Remove from stove. Add vanilla and walnuts. Stir gently until mixture becomes creamy. Turn out onto greased platter. Separate the nuts as they cool.

Grocery List *

Assorted fruit juices | Tomatoes
   for punch | Cottage cheese
Box of strawberries | Brown-and-serve rolls

Mint
Tuna
Noodles
Cheese
Lettuce

Eggs
Strawberry ice cream
Walnuts
Orange juice

* *Does not include staples.*

AFTER-LUNCH FUN

Don't worry too much about entertainment for a group of this sort because they're as sociable as a basket of kittens! However, here are a few games and contests that are fun.

BABY CONTEST

This promises to be one of the high spots of the party if you are able to assemble the "props." Advance preparations:

The game committee collects a baby picture from each guest and mounts all the pictures on a large piece of construction paper with a number over each one. Keep the display covered until ready to use it.

Pencils and papers are distributed, the contest is explained, and the exhibit unveiled.

Guests try to identify the baby pictures, and the one who guesses the greatest number correctly, wins. It is best to have two prizes in case of a tie. On the same sheet is a space where, before the pictures are identified, one votes for the prettiest baby.

HUNT FOR THE WORD

Preparations ahead of time:

The game committee prints the following words on a piece of paper, then attaches a number to each letter in a word.

MOTHER   DIAPER
FATHER   PABLUM
DOCTOR   BOTTLE
BUNDLE   SHOWER
WEIGHT   CRADLE

For instance, the word "Doctor" would be printed like this:

D 3   O 3   C 3   T 3   O 3   R 3

Then cut the letters apart and hide them around the living room. Guests draw for a number, then the search is on for the six letters in her word. First one to find the slips and to correctly assemble the word, wins.

MANY HAPPY RETURNS OF THE DAY

Telegram game. Each contestant draws a letter from a hat. She then must compose a ten-word telegram announcing the baby's birth, using the letter she has drawn to start each word.

Example:

CUTE CHEERFULLY CUDDLY

CHARMING CHERUB CALLED

CONNIE COOS CONSTANTLY

CONTENTEDLY.

A LOOK INTO THE FUTURE

Preparations ahead of time:

The game committee types a sheet for each guest asking the following questions:

Sue's baby will be born on?

Hour?

Boy or girl?

Twins?

Triplets?

Weight?

Color of hair?

Behavior?

Name?

What will the baby look like?

(PORTRAIT HERE)

Each contestant signs her name, and the one whose description is closest wins. Although the prize will be on display, it will obviously have to be awarded later.

PRESENTING THE GIFTS

You will now want an effective container for the gifts. Any of the following would be suitable: a bassinet, an antique cradle, a decorated baby buggy, or a decorated clothes basket.

Since so many of the gifts are likely to be on the bulky side, you may decide to fold a large sheet like a diaper, place the gifts inside, and secure it with a tremendous safety pin; then drag the bundle unceremoniously into the room.

FORTUNES

As the gifts are assembled, each one will be tied to one end of a long ribbon—each ribbon being of a different color. At the other end is tied a fortune. (The fortunes are made up and attached to the gifts by the gift committee before the party.) All the fortunes are piled together in front of Sue. She selects a fortune, reads it, and then opens the present which is at the end of it. You can imagine the screams of anguish from the donors.

Samples:

For you I see a household piled
With 14 children, loud and wild,

Two birds, a cat, a wire-haired terrier,
But remember, dear, the more the merrier.

A happy girl you'll always be,
You won the heart that loves but thee,
Children galore, around you buzzing,
Oh well, they're cheaper by the dozen!

Your fate will be a travellin' man,
A lady killer, a Dapper Dan,
Beware, my dear, for you will find
When out of sight, then out of mind.

More rhyming fortunes

For you I see a life of joy,
Six strapping girls and one small boy.

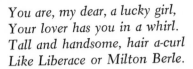

You'll soon be shopping for safety pins,
For you I see two sets of twins.

If I can read aright your fate
Within a year three changes great.
Names of triplets? Let me see,
Tom, Dick and Mary Lee.

You are pretty, and sweet, with manner gra-
cious,
When your beau's not around, you are often
flirtatious!

Sugar and spice, all babies are nice,
Angels two I see for you.

My advice to you, my dear, take heed:
In controlling men
If you don't at first succeed
Cry, cry again.

You are, my dear, a lucky girl,
Your lover has you in a whirl.
Tall and handsome, hair a-curl
Like Liberace or Milton Berle.

You'll travel in Michigan, Kansas, and
Maine,
With pleasure your days will be rife,
'Neath Florida's palms
You'll meet a bold swain
Who'll persuade you to try wedded life.

AN EXTRA GIFT

What's in the basket?

Each girl has been requested to bring a small extra gift, costing not more than 50 cents. These are placed in a basket and numbered. Two gifts are to be opened each day at the hospital. Which gift is to be opened which day will be marked on the outside of the package.

These gifts could be items such as guest soaps, sachets, notepaper, handkerchiefs, miniature jars of homemade jam, pocket novels, etc.

It would give an added touch to have the basket decorated with appropriate symbols for the month in which the baby is expected. For instance, gay Valentines for February, shamrocks for March, chenille chicks for Eastertime, and so forth.

In order to avoid confusion, this little gift basket could be taken to the hospital on the second day.

Coffee royal brunch

(*A perfect party to give on Sundays or special holidays*)

All of us like to go to a party that's different. This one had so many worthwhile features that I'd like to tell you about it.

Madeline patterned it somewhat after the cocktail party, but in my opinion it was much more fun. Guests dropped in informally between 11 and 2, and the menu was planned to appeal to breakfasters and lunchers alike.

THE FLOWING BOWL

After a warm welcome at the door, and after wraps were disposed of, Neil escorted us to a self-service punchbowl brimming with Coffee Royal. This is a happy combination of strong coffee, dark rum, and vanilla ice cream. It's easy to make as you go along, and oh, so delicious!

About thirty-five guests were expected, so our hosts had set up a duplicate punch service in the library. Small groups were able to visit in the vicinity of the "flowing bowl"

61

without undue crowding. On another table Neil had thoughtfully provided a pitcher of iced fruit juice for those who preferred it.

I believe host and guests alike favor the "self-service" idea. It keeps guests circulating, and it relieves the host for the more important duties of visiting with his guests and making sure that no one is stranded.

RELAXED AND EASY ATMOSPHERE

Because of the hour and the fact that it was a holiday, people seemed to be in a particularly relaxed and gay mood. No one appeared to be in a hurry to go on somewhere else, and small groups sat around enjoying leisurely conversation.

SPRINGTIME BUFFET TABLE

Madeline's buffet was a festive sight indeed. She had covered her dining table with a luscious raspberry-colored cloth. It was of Indianhead, and she had made it herself.

An antique white birdcage, overflowing with spring flowers and trailing vines, made a graceful centerpiece. This was flanked by a pair of handsome white ceramic roosters, fresh from the kiln of the hostess. Plates, cups, and saucers were of the most delicate porcelain; the pattern was a white background with a spray of spring flowers in vibrant colors.

Food was kept hot in chafing dishes and in casseroles over candle warmers. Hot breads and coffee were replenished often by a party maid. The coffee service, cups, and saucers were set up on a convenient Welsh cupboard, with a plate of hot miniature caramel nut rolls nearby.

Guests were invited to serve themselves whenever they wished. Food could be eaten standing informally around the table, or if anyone preferred, a plate could be filled and carried into another room. The advantage of this arrangement was that the table was never too crowded at any one time.

An informal table set for an autumn brunch is shown on the facing page.

Photo by Syzdek; table setting by B. Altman & Co.

Brunch

Buffet

Autumn

Table

CLOTH   Dark-brown linen

NAPKINS   Yellow linen

CHINA   California Provincial pottery by Poppy Trail. There are shades of red and brown and a touch of yellow in the rooster design. Mugs, sugar, creamer, salt-and-pepper set are orangey red.

SILVER   Wooden-handled

CENTERPIECE   Antique iron pot with long handle is used as a container for autumn leaves and dried grasses. An antique wrought-iron doorstop in a wheat pattern harmonizes with the autumn theme.

SERVING DISHES   Coffee mill in upper left-hand corner is used for cheese and crackers. The drawer partially opened is filled with crackers, and cubes of cheese are attached to "cheese mice" picks in a variety of colors. The glass cover for the roll dish is available separately.

menu

Use any of your favorite breakfast and luncheon specialties, or choose from among these:

On a toothpick

Codfish balls (*the frozen kind*) *heated*

French fried potato balls

Chafing dish

Creamed chicken for tiny buttered biscuits

* Sausage Stroganoff (*a dunk for Melba toast*)

Breads

Toasted English muffins, with choice of jams

Quick carmel-nut rolls (*use the brown-and-serve variety*)

Finger foods

* Mushrooms stuffed with toasted crumbs and crisp bacon bits

* Crab Tarts à la Bernice

* Stuffed eggs, with curry seasoning and chopped peanuts

For that sweet tooth

* Irene's shortbread cookies

* Cinnamon snails

Danish pastry

* See recipe section for starred items.

RECISE

SAUSAGE STROGANOFF

1 clove garlic
2 lb. bulk sausage
3 tbsp. flour
2 cups milk
⅛ lb. butter or
   margarine
2 large onions
   sliced, then
   chopped

1 can mushrooms
2 tsp. soy sauce
2 tbsp. Worcester-
   shire sauce
   salt, pepper, and
   paprika
1 pint commercial
   sour cream

Rub large skillet with garlic and heat.

Brown the sausage well. Pour off the grease as it accumulates.

Dredge the sausage with the flour. Add milk and simmer until slightly thickened. Set aside.

Sauté the onions and mushrooms in butter.

To the cream sauce mixture, add the soy sauce, Worcestershire sauce, onions, and mushrooms. When the mixture bubbles, add the sour cream. Keep hot in chafing dish. Heap up on little biscuits or use as a dunk for Melba toast.

MUSHROOMS STUFFED WITH TOASTED CRUMBS AND BACON BITS

Mushrooms (Allow
   2 medium ones
   per person)
2 cups dry bread
   crumbs

⅛ pound butter
Lawry's Seasoned Salt
½ lb. bacon

Remove stems from mushrooms. Scrub the caps with a soft brush. Turn upside down and drain thoroughly between paper towels.

With scissors or sharp knife, slice bacon into ½ inch strips. (Slice straight across the bacon as it comes from the package.) Cook until crisp. (Pieces will separate as they cook.) Drain on paper towels. Pour off bacon grease and store.

Melt butter in pan. Add bread crumbs and brown.

Add bacon to bread crumbs and work them together lightly with your fingers.

Spoon the mixture into the mushrooms, and press into the caps. Sprinkle the tops with Lawry's Seasoned Salt.

Broil until lightly browned.

COFFEE ROYAL

1 gallon strong coffee
1 gallon vanilla ice cream
1 quart dark rum

Mix the chilled coffee and rum together.

Just before serving time, add the ice cream.

Serve in punchbowl. Punch cups or small glasses are about the right size for individual portions.

CRAB TARTS À LA BERNICE

½ cup mayonnaise
¼ tsp. salt
¼ tsp. Tabasco
1 tsp. Worcester-
shire sauce
1 tsp. lemon juice
½ tsp. paprika
1 tbsp. horseradish

1 clove garlic, minced
or put through gar-
lic press
1 can crabmeat
(6 oz.)
1 box piecrust mix, or
your favorite recipe
Parmesan cheese

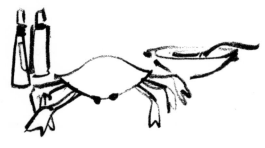

1. Mix the first eight ingredients and allow to stand for several hours.
2. Make favorite pastry recipe or use one package of prepared mix. Roll as for pie crust; cut circles with small biscuit cutter.
3. Mix crabmeat with the seasoned mayonnaise mixture, reserving one quarter of the mayonnaise.
4. Place ½ tsp. of crabmeat mixture in the center of each pastry round. Fold over to form half-circle. Press edges together and seal securely with tines of fork. Prick top once with fork. The tarts may be frozen or stored in icebox for several hours.
5. Just before baking, brush with remaining mayonnaise. Sprinkle with paprika or Parmesan cheese.
6. Bake in 450-degree oven for 20 minutes. If frozen, longer baking is necessary. Serve hot. Yields 25–30 tarts.

STUFFED EGGS WITH CURRY SEASONING AND CHOPPED PEANUTS

1 doz. hard-cooked eggs
1¼ cups mayonnaise or boiled dressing
Salt and pepper to taste
2 tsp. curry powder
½ cup finely chopped peanuts

Remove shells from eggs. Cut in half lengthwise. Mash the yolks with the remaining ingredients. Restuff eggs.

(These can be prepared in advance. Arrange the eggs on plate or platter, then cover the whole thing with Saran Wrap to prevent drying.

IRENE'S SHORTBREAD COOKIES

3 cups flour
1 cup sugar, preferably confectioner's sugar
½ lb. margarine or butter (1 cup)

Cream together butter and sugar. Beat very well until fluffy. Add flour gradually, and beat well after each addition. Chill thoroughly in icebox. Roll in balls about the size of a small egg, then flatten a little. If you wish, dot small pieces of maraschino cherry on top. Place on ungreased cookie sheet 1 inch apart. Bake at 350 degrees for 30 minutes, or until lightly browned.

CINNAMON SNAILS

1 pkg. piecrust mix
1 tbsp. cinnamon
3 tbsp. sugar

Mix together the sugar and cinnamon. Set aside.

Roll pastry thin. Sprinkle cinnamon-sugar mixture generously all over the top. Roll up and seal the edges by pinching together with fingers.

With sharp knife, cut into ½-inch slices. Bake in 400-degree oven about 10 minutes until browned.

Self-service cocktail party

"Honey, Doris and Charles are coming through on their way East, and I think it would be fun to have a cocktail party for them so they can see all their old friends."

or

"Do you realize we graduated almost ten years ago? Let's get the gang together and plan a class reunion."

or

"You know, today at the office, it occurred to me that we've never had the office force here. Do you think we could swing a cocktail party?"

There are times for all of us when we want to entertain a large group of people at one time. The best solution is a cocktail party, either nonalcoholic or otherwise.

EAT, DRINK, AND BE MERRY

NONALCOHOLIC DRINKS

Fruit Punch   Clam Juice

Egg Nog   Tomato Juice

Apple Cider   Coffee

ALCOHOLIC DRINKS

* Martinis

* Manhattans

Scotch and bourbon with choice of mixes

Serve any or all of these

* Devilled Clams   * Mac's Cheese Wafers

* Paper-thin Filet Steak

Rolls, Piquant Sauce

* Roquefort-Bacon-Parsley Spread
on slices of icebox rye bread

Chicken à la King in Chafing Dish
served on tiny pastry circles

* Anne's Hawaiian Meatballs

Cheese Rarebit in Chafing Dish served on
crisp crackers

* Caviar and cream cheese à la Julie

* Starred items will be found in recipe section.

If you don't want to serve such an elaborate spread, set out various kinds of crackers and cheese, potato chips, prepared cream cheese dips, Fritos, sliced cold meats, small buns, and relishes. This is certainly enough, particularly if the cocktail party precedes another affair at which food is to be served.

COCKTAIL PARTIES THE EASY WAY

SELF-SERVICE BAR

Preliminary preparations:

Spread a plastic cloth on a dinette table or other sturdy surface.

Cover it with a white cotton or linen cloth which has a generous overhang on all sides.

Above the table tack a sign approximately 24 by 5 inches reading SELF-SERVICE BAR.

On the table set the following

Scotch	Long bar spoon
Bourbon or rye	2 Jiggers
Ice tongs (optional)	Bottle opener

Glasses for mixed drinks	Rubber tops
Glasses for cocktails	Cocktail napkins

Mixers

Ginger ale	Water
Soda	Coca-Cola

Garnishes (any or all of these)

Maraschino cherries	Lemon twists
Cocktail onions	Lime slices
Stuffed olives	Orange slices

Just before the party, set out ice in an ice bucket. Also have a bar towel nearby.

COCKTAILS

In addition, you may want to serve a choice of cocktails. Manhattans and Martinis are favorites and may be made several hours in advance and chilled thoroughly in refrigerator.

To make Manhattans

Combine 3 parts bourbon
       1 part Sweet Vermouth
       3 dashes Angostura bitters

To make Martinis

Combine from 3 to 5 parts gin (according to taste)
       1 part Dry Vermouth
Stir, do not shake.

At party time

Add a few ice cubes for dilution. Set filled cocktail shakers or pitchers on the Self-service Bar, or on a tray with cocktail glasses in another location. Nearby, place a bowl of cherries on picks for the Manhattans, and bowls of olives, cocktail onions, and pieces of lemon peel for the Martinis.

ADVANTAGES OF "SERVE-YOURSELF" SYSTEM

1. It enables the host and hostess to circulate among their friends and join the fun.

2. It keeps the guests circulating.

3. By setting out the drinks in more than one place, it is possible to eliminate any bottlenecks around the bar.

4. Guests have no more or less than they want. (A suggestion at this point to over-hospitable hosts. Don't insist on giving guests more to drink than they want.)

QUESTIONS AND ANSWERS

How many drinks will a fifth make?

About fifteen to twenty, depending on strength desired.

How many drinks will the average guest have?

Two or three. Plan for about one drink per 30 minutes per person.

How much of a choice should the host provide?

Two cocktails and either bourbon or Scotch should be ample. Always have a nonalcoholic drink on hand as well.

How much does a drink cost?

In your home, about 30 cents.

How many different types of glasses should one have?

Three should be enough—6- or 8-ounce tumblers for mixed drinks such as bourbon and soda
cocktail glasses (about 4 oz.)
old fashioned glasses (about 6 oz.)

Can you use an inexpensive brand of liquor in cocktails?

No. Serve liquor of good quality.

ODDS AND ENDS

Ice. It is better to have too much ice than not enough. Ice dealers usually have available both cubes and chipped ice, and it is not expensive. Don't hesitate to get ice ahead of time; a large bag lasts for hours, especially if it is kept covered. (I usually keep it wrapped in a blanket near the back door, and refill ice buckets as necessary. If an ice dealer is not available, make ice ahead of time and store in the freezer. If you do not have a deep freeze, you may have friendly neighbors who will come to the rescue beforehand (not frantically in the middle of the party).

Size of glasses. When you serve mixed drinks, it is better to serve them in a small, 6- or 8-ounce glass than in a very tall one. If drinks are served in large glasses, they may get weak and warm before you can finish them.

YOUR TABLE

There is a wide range of possibilities here. I've seen cocktail buffet tables set with a handsome lace cloth and silver candelabra, and I've seen them set in the most casual manner with a checkered gingham cloth and pottery accessories.

Whether your choice is formal or informal, make it as festive as possible with flowers and candles. Your food, attractively and temptingly displayed, will be the most intriguing decoration.

CHECK-OFF LIST

Cloth
Small napkins
Small plates (optional)
Centerpiece
Candles
Salt and pepper shakers
Serving forks and spoons
Serving dishes, chafing dishes, etc.

RECEPTIONS ▓▓▓▓▓▓▓▓▓▓▓

DEVILLED CLAMS

from "A Cook's Tour of Quantico" for 50

100 Little Neck clams
2 large green peppers
1 large Spanish onion
1 stalk celery
¾ lb. butter
2 tbsp. dry mustard
1 tsp. red pepper
1 tbsp. Worcestershire sauce
1 tbsp. Tabasco
1 qt. cracker meal
2 cups flour
2 eggs beaten (Set aside)

Steam clams in ¾ cup water in covered pot 12 minutes. Remove clams from shells and chop finely. Save broth. Save shells.

Chop finely the green peppers, onion, and celery, and sauté them in the butter for 30 minutes. Add chopped clams. Add the mustard, red pepper, Worcestershire sauce, Tabasco, cracker meal, and flour. Use clam broth to thin roux, but the mixture must be very thick. Let stand and cool for 3 hours. Fill each shell with mixture. Dip the filled part in beaten egg or a thin batter, then cover with bread crumbs and cook in deep fat fryer at 350 degrees until brown. Remove and serve at once.

This recipe involves the most work, but is well worth the extra trouble. It is a real gourmet dish. Place the clams on a tray to serve, with a supply of napkins and cocktail forks or small plastic forks.

MAC'S CHEESE WAFERS

½ lb. grated cheese (rat cheese or black rind cheddar)
1½ cups flour
¼ lb. butter
½ tsp. salt
¼ tsp. red pepper
¼ tsp. paprika

Mix together, then add 1½ cups flour.
Mix well with hands, and shape into a roll, about 2 inches in diameter.
Wrap in waxed paper and put in refrigerator until ready to bake.
Slice and bake on cookie sheet 10 minutes at 350 degrees. If you wish, put a salted pecan in center of each before baking. Serve hot or cold.

CAVIAR AND CREAM CHEESE
À LA JULIE

Soften two large packages of cream cheese with cream.
Add 2 tbsp. grated onion.
Beat until very smooth, and form into a ball on a plate.
Spoon black caviar over the cream cheese

mixture until it is completely covered. (Work gently with the caviar to avoid bruising it.) Pile Ritz crackers around the outer edge. Provide butter knife for spreading.

In order to avoid two cream cheese mixtures you will probably want to make a choice between this and the Roquefort–bacon–parsley recipe. Each is so good that I couldn't resist giving both recipes.

PAPER-THIN FILET STEAK ROLLS WITH PIQUANT SAUCE

Here is a hearty cocktail snack, noted not only for its delicious taste, but for the note of glamour introduced as it is cooked at the table. You will need for equipment an electric frying pan and a chafing dish for the sauce.

Let me give you the sauce recipe first, as sauce may be made in advance.

Piquant sauce (to serve 12)

4 tbsp. finely chopped sweet pickle
4 tbsp. finely chopped onion
2 tbsp. finely chopped parsley
3 cups salad dressing
2 tbsp. Worcestershire sauce
½ tsp. marjoram
½ tsp. paprika
6 tbsp. soy sauce or Brown-Quick
6 tbsp. ketchup
4 drops Tabasco sauce

Mix well together and store in refrigerator. Heat in top of chafing dish before serving.

And now for the steak

Have the butcher slice filet mignon in paper-thin slices. Arrange these on a large plate next to the electric frying pan on a table or shelf. Heat the pan to temperature indicated on the handle, approximately 420 degrees. Grease the pan slightly with a salad oil (rather than margarine or butter, as oil will not smoke). Have nearby thin slices of very fresh buttered bread from which the crusts have been cut. Cook the steaks very quickly, first on one side, then the other, dip in the sauce, then place on a piece of bread, roll up, and eat.

If you're among good friends, make each person cook his own.

ANNE'S HAWAIIAN MEATBALLS

2 cans meatballs (Boy-ar-dee's)
1 can drained crushed pineapple

Combine meatballs, gravy, and pineapple. Keep hot in top of chafing dish. Provide toothpicks with which to spear them.

ROQUEFORT–BACON–PARSLEY SPREAD ON SLICES OF ICEBOX RYE BREAD

Approximately 1 lb. Roquefort cheese
2 large pkgs. cream cheese
Fresh ground pepper
1 clove garlic, put through press
1 tbsp. grated onion
1 tbsp. Worcestershire sauce
1 tsp. celery salt
½ lb. bacon
1 bunch parsley
2 loaves icebox rye bread

With scissors, cut bacon into thin strips crosswise and fry until crisp. Set aside.

Remove stems from parsley. Cut the florets into tiny pieces with scissors. Set aside.

Mash the Roquefort and cream cheese; add a little milk or cream to make it of spreading consistency. Add pepper, garlic, grated onion, Worcestershire sauce, and celery salt. Beat well until smooth.

Heap it on a salad plate, making a smooth mound. Arrange bacon and parsley in alternate stripes over the mound of cheese.

Set salad plate on dinner or service plate and arrange buttered rye slices around the edge. Provide butter knife for spreading.

easy **M** exican
supper

5:30 You walk in the door with your guests after the big football game (or whatever).

Turn the oven to a temperature of 425 degrees.

Spread the topping upon your casserole.

5:45 Pop the casserole into the oven, and rejoin your guests for cocktails and snacks.

6:15 Make coffee and salad.

6:30 Call your guests to supper.

The whole dinner is as easy as that, and oh, so delicious!

The single girl or man could give this party easily, with the help of one other person to serve the cocktails and to act as host during the few minutes that the chef is in the kitchen.

After the exhilaration of a matinee or a sporting event, it is fun to extend the companionship into the evening.

The following menu is so planned that there will be a minimum of last-minute preparations. (The trick is to make the tamale pie and the dessert in the morning, or even on the preceding day.)

> *Menu*
>
> * *Frosty Tequila Cocktails*
>
> *Mexican Broad Beans and Pepitas (nibblers)*
>
> * *Mary's Easy Tamale Pie*
>
> * *Guacamole Salad*
>
> *Beer (optional)*
>
> * *Natilla (custard with caramel sauce)*
>
> *Coffee*
>
> * *Starred items will be found in recipe section.*

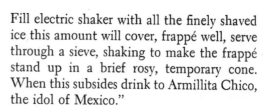

While you are preparing the casserole, maybe your best beau would whip up some delicious Tequila Cocktails.

FROSTY TEQUILA COCKTAILS

This recipe was found in the Gentleman's Companion Exotic Drink Book *by Charles H. Baker, Jr. (Crown Publishers, Inc., 1946).*

Here is the recipe in his words:
"Tequila, 3 jiggers
Limes, strained juice 2
Orange-flower water 2 dashes
Grenadine, dash, for color

Fill electric shaker with all the finely shaved ice this amount will cover, frappé well, serve through a sieve, shaking to make the frappé stand up in a brief rosy, temporary cone. When this subsides drink to Armillita Chico, the idol of Mexico."

The Mexican Broad Beans which I mentioned, and the Pepitas (salted pumpkin seeds), are now available at almost all specialty food shops, and in many cases at the corner grocery store. I think you'll like them.

MARY'S EASY TAMALE PIE

For 4:
- 1 lb. chopped beef
- 1 medium chopped onion
- 1 medium chopped green pepper
- 2 cans tomato sauce
- 2 cloves garlic, minced or put through garlic press
- 1 tbsp. chili powder
- 1–2 flakes red pepper, crushed
- 1 large can kidney beans
- 1 pkg. Flako corn-muffin mix

Brown the meat. Add other ingredients except beans.

Cook 30 minutes over low heat, stirring often. Add beans and remove from heat.

In the meantime make cornmeal muffin batter, according to directions on the package.

Put batter on top of bean and meat mixture, and bake 30 to 40 minutes until top is browned. Serve very hot.

(If you make this up ahead of time, store the meat mixture in refrigerator. Put muffin batter on top just before baking.

I believe it would be a good idea to make two pies. This will allow for generous "seconds."

GUACAMOLE SALAD

You will need per person:
- ½ avocado
- ½ ripe tomato
- ½ sliced hard-boiled egg
- ½ tender green onion
- Salad greens

Lime dressing

- ¼ cup olive oil
- ½ cup lime juice
- 1 tsp. salt
- 1 tsp. sugar
- 1½ tsp. Worcestershire sauce
- 1 garlic clove, minced fine
- ½ tsp. fresh ground pepper

Shake vigorously. Make at least one day before using.

To arrange salad

Arrange a bed of salad greens on large plate or platter.

Cut each avocado in half, remove the pit, and arrange on salad greens.

Slice tiny green onions very fine. Sprinkle on avocado.

Arrange wedges of tomato and hard-boiled egg around edge.

Guests apply their own dressing at serving time.

NATILLA

(*This recipe is in* Favorite Recipes from the United Nations, *published by the United States Committee for the United Nations, Washington, D.C.*)

It is similar to Crème Brûlée.

4 cups milk
6 egg yolks beaten slightly
½ cup sugar
½ cup sifted flour
¼ tsp. salt
1 tsp. vanilla
½ cup light brown sugar

Scald 3 cups of milk in top of a double boiler. Mix sugar, flour, and salt, and stir in 1 cup of cold milk and egg yolks; add mixture to scalded milk.

Continue cooking over boiling water, stirring constantly until thick. Remove from heat, let stand a few minutes, then add the vanilla. Pour custard into a shallow glass baking dish. When custard is entirely cold, sprinkle brown sugar generously over the top. Be sure sugar is free of lumps. Then place the baking dish beneath the broiler until the sugar caramelizes all over the top. Be sure that the flame does not touch the sides of the dish. Let stand in the refrigerator for several hours before serving, so that the caramelized sugar forms a sauce on top of the custard. Yield: 6 servings.

INVITATIONS

SALUDO

To carry out the theme even further, you might send invitations written in Spanish, with the English translation inside.

> Saludo
> Ud. está invitada a una cena mexicana a la casa de los Stacy, el viernes, veinte de enero, a las siete de la tarde.
> Haga el favor de telefonear para decirnos si Ud. podrá asistir.

which means:

Greetings:

You are invited to a Mexican supper at the home of the Stacys at six o'clock on Friday night, the 20th of January.

Please be kind enough to call and let us know if you can come.

Photo by Syzdek; table setting by B. Altman & Co.

Easy

Mexican

Supper

CLOTH Striped beach towel (to resemble serape)

NAPKINS Yellow linen

CHINA Harkerware White Cap design (off-white pottery with pearl-gray edge)

SILVER Stainless steel (pattern Cora)

GLASSWARE Square tumblers in dark green

CENTERPIECE Woven basket, with vegetables in the bottom section, corn muffins in upper section

CANDLES Tall red tapers. Holders are fresh green peppers, upside down, with a small hole cut in each so that candle will fit securely.

SERVING DISHES Covered casserole and salad bowl are of pottery. Salad servers are wooden with ceramic handles.

RED, WHITE, AND GREEN TABLE

One of my friends who specializes in Mexican food uses the national colors of Mexico in the color scheme for her table.

CLOTH. Made of yard goods. Has a black background, with a Mexican-Indian border print in red, white, and green. (Cost of cloth, under $3.00.)

NAPKINS. Red cotton.

CHINA. White, small platters and cups and saucers with fluted edges, available in open stock from the ten-cent store.

GLASSWARE. Bright green Mexican goblets, hand blown (approximately 49 cents each).

CANDLESTICKS. Green peppers, hollowed out. Secure candles in melted candle wax. Use two or three on each side of centerpiece.

CENTERPIECE. Red peppers, white onions, and green peppers arranged at random on tablecloth on center of table. Tuck twigs, green leaves here and there.

PLACE CARDS. Plain white ones, on which are written SENOR STACY, SENORA STACY, SENOR DUPLANTIS, SENORA DUPLANTIS, SENOR WELCH, SENORA WELCH.

An alternate and equally festive Mexican table is illustrated on the facing page.

SUGGESTIONS ON SERVING

1. Place the tamale pie, salad, salad dressing, and plates on the buffet. Guests serve themselves, then find their places at the table.
2. Place the dessert and coffee service on a serving table or teacart near the hostess.

3. When guests have finished the main course, they will pass their plates to the hostess who will place them on the bottom shelf of the serving table. In this way, the hostess can remain seated at the table throughout the meal.

MUSIC

Not really necessary, but a touch that would give added enjoyment, would be a long-playing record of beautiful Mexican music.

GROCERY LIST

Limes
Mexican broad
  beans
Pepitas
Chopped beef
Onions
Green pepper
Tomato sauce
Garlic
Kidney beans

Flako corn-muffin
  mix
Avocados
Tomatoes
Eggs
Salad greens
Green onions
Milk
Coffee
Tequila

Japanese Sukiyaki dinner

A DINNER IN JAPAN

Stars over Tokyo; what an unforgettable sight! Beneath us the twinkling lights of that tremendous city extended as far as we could see.

The Japanese home to which we had been invited was beautifully located on the side of a hill, surrounded by gardens and walks. We paused on the veranda for a few moments to take advantage of the breath-taking views from every side.

At the door we removed our shoes as is the Japanese custom. Soft slippers were offered to us which added to our comfort and to the informality of the evening.

Having never been in a Japanese home before, I was much interested in the way it was designed and furnished. I noticed a certain resemblance to contemporary Western homes.

Sliding walls between the living rooms and gardens permitted easy passage between indoor and outdoor areas. The rooms were airy and uncluttered, and sparsely but tastefully decorated. A desk, some bookshelves, a low table over which hung the traditional Japanese lanterns, and bright-colored floor

80

cushions constituted the furniture in the first room to which we were shown. A tall oriental vase with a riotous arrangement of cherry blossoms was placed on the floor in front of a large window. On the small table was a very simple but effective flower arrangement.

Floors were completely covered by straw mats over heavy padding. These were bound and joined together by gaily patterned silk tape. When we walked on them we noticed they had a delightfully springy feeling underfoot.

Our host led us to a large inner room where the dinner party was to take place. There were three sets of tables.

All the tables were low, not more than 14 inches high. We sat on surprisingly comfortable woven cushions—quite large ones (about 18 inches in diameter) slightly hollow in the center.

At the first table we were served the traditional Japanese drink, a rice wine called Sake. It was warmed slightly and then poured from a beautifully designed porcelain decanter into delicate porcelain cups.

Presently we moved on to a second table which was designed in a half-circle. We sat on cushions facing the cook who presided at a brazier, cooking and serving the Shrimp Tempura. We were served one shrimp at a time, golden brown, still sizzling hot and exquisitely tender. We would scarcely have time to eat one when another would be placed on the plate, each one more delicious than the last. Each of us was supplied with a small bowl of sauce in which to dip the shrimp. (Tempura is such a favorite in Japan that there are famous restaurants specializing in this one dish alone.)

From there we moved to the third table, much like the first in form but slightly wider. In the center was a Hibachi—a charcoal brazier over which a heavy iron skillet

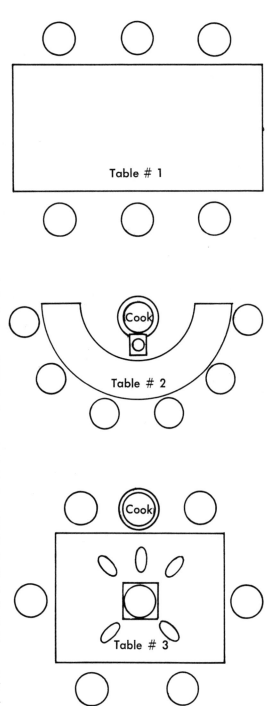

fits snugly. The cook half kneels behind it, and cooks the Sukiyaki right before the eyes of the guests. Small platters of finely cut vegetables and meat were arranged artistically around the Hibachi. The combination of colors and the precise way the meat and vegetables had been cut made a beautiful picture.

When the correct temperature was reached, the cook rendered a little beef suet in the heavy deep skillet and added the shoestring strips of beef to brown. He turned it once to brown the other side, added the sauce and the vegetables, and cooked everything together for about 10 minutes. The Japanese like their vegetables crisp—just barely cooked—and this is what gives the delightful contrast in texture.

The Sukiyaki was served direct from the pot to our bowls. Each of us had a small cup of beaten egg in which to dip the meat. The heat of the meat cooks the egg just enough, and gives it a delightful flavor. Rice was served too, and great quantities of tea.

During the evening we were entertained by three Japanese girls beautifully gowned in exotic kimonos and obis. They danced and sang to the accompaniment of a lutelike instrument; they were, moreover, excellent conversationalists and gay as butterflies.

It was truly an evening to remember.

SUKIYAKI DINNER AT HOME

Very few of us have Hibachis or any of the other equipment mentioned before, but that needn't prevent us from giving a Japanese dinner. As a matter of fact you can serve this unusual and delicious meal at home with greater ease than can the Japanese by putting your wonderful electrical appliances to work. An electric deep-fat fryer, with its controlled temperature, is perfect for the Shrimp Tempura. And for the Sukiyaki itself, what could be better than your heat-controlled electric frying pan? Or you could use a deep heavy skillet or Dutch oven over a hot plate, the method used at the well-known Miyako Japanese restaurant in New York City. It's such fun at a party to see the food cooked in front of you, and such a boon to the hostess to be able to do it this way.

Menu

* Butterfly Shrimp Tempura

* Mustard Sauce

*Sukiyaki, Shoyu Sauce   Boiled Rice

*Salad of Spinach
with Sesame Seed Dressing

Watermelon Pickles

*Tangerine Sections in Cocoanut Syrup

Oolong Tea

* Starred items will be found in the recipe section.

RECICES

BUTTERFLY SHRIMP TEMPURA

You will need:

Approximately 5–6 large shrimp per person

A bowl of flour

Thin batter

Oil for deep frying; this can be peanut oil, cottonseed oil, lard or hydrogenated fat. The melted fat must be deep enough so that the food can be submerged.

Sauce for dipping

Preparation of shrimp. Clean shrimp. Slit along the outside curvature without cutting all the way through. Flatten each to resemble a butterfly.

Recipe for thin batter
(*From* Shrimp Cookery, *by Helen Worth.*)

2 eggs	½ cup sifted flour
½ cup milk	½ tsp. salt
4 tbsp. melted butter	½ tsp. sugar

Beat the eggs well.

Beat in the milk and melted butter.

Sift the flour with the salt and sugar.

Combine liquid and dry ingredients and beat smooth.

And now you are ready to deep-fry. First you heat the fat to 375 degrees, or until a 1-inch cube of white bread will become light brown in 40 seconds. It is important to have the fat at the right temperature. If it's too hot, the shrimp cooks too quickly on the outside, and not enough on the inside. If the temperature is too low, the food absorbs too much fat and is greasy.

Dip shrimp in flour, then into batter, then into the fat. Don't overload the kettle. Five or six shrimp at a time should be about right. As soon as they are light brown on one side, turn with a slotted spoon or tongs. Brown the other side, and drain a moment on paper towels. Serve hot.

A sauce similar to the one the Japanese use is made by combining ¼ cup soy sauce, ½ cup sherry, 1 tsp. sugar, 1 tbsp. grated ginger and/or ½ grated white turnip.

I believe, however, that the following mustard sauce is more appealing to the American palate:

Blend together:

½ cup prepared mustard

½ cup salad dressing

½ cup Heinz ketchup

¼ cup soy sauce

SUKIYAKI
(*pronounced SKEE YA' KEE*)

The following recipe is an American version of the dish. My Japanese cookbook calls for such items as bean curd, burdock root, Sake, Shirataki. These are seldom seen at the corner market. So we've made some substitutions, and the result is very good eating.

For 6 people you will need:

1½ lb. tender steak, cut paper-thin by your butcher

A piece of beef suet, or 2 tbsp. fat. (Do not use butter or margarine.)

2 large onions cut fine

4 green onions, cut in 1-inch lengths

2 stalks celery cut diagonally in 1-inch lengths

Mushrooms, ½ lb. Cut straight through the cap and stem in ¼-inch slices.

1 cup bamboo shoots, cut in shoestring strips

Sauce

½ cup soy sauce (Japanese call it "shoyu")

2 tbsp. sugar

½ cup chicken or beef stock or bouillon cube in ½ cup water

2 tbsp. sherry

Keep each vegetable separate. Arrange them around the meat on a large platter, or in separate bowls.

Heat skillet until very hot. Render the suet a little, or add the fat.

Brown the meat on both sides.

Add the sauce.

Add the vegetables in layers.

Cook 5 minutes at high heat, then simmer covered for 5 to 10 minutes more. (The vegetables must be *just* done.)

Optional. A small bowl of beaten eggs at each place in which to dunk the meat.

SALAD OF SPINACH WITH SESAME SEED DRESSING

Dressing

4 tbsp. white sesame seeds (available now in most supermarkets)

4 tbsp. vinegar

4 tbsp. sugar

1 tbsp. soy sauce

Brown the sesame seeds in a frying pan until light brown.

Add the other ingredients.

To serve: Place a plate of spinach leaves and an individual bowl of dressing in front of each diner. He dips the spinach into the dressing.

TANGERINE SECTIONS IN COCOANUT SYRUP

6 tangerines	2 cups water
1 cup sugar	1 cup cocoanut

Separate tangerine sections. Place them in kettle with sugar, water and cocoanut. Boil gently 5 minutes uncovered.

Cool and serve in sherbet glasses.

GROCERY LIST *

Large shrimp	Celery
Peanut oil or other fat	Mushrooms
for deep frying	Spinach

* Does not include staples.

Soy sauce	Bamboo shoots
Steak or other tender beef	Sesame seeds
Onions	Tangerines
Green onions	Cocoanut

INVITATIONS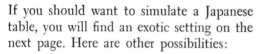

I use Japanese notepaper for invitations to a Sukiyaki party. Mine has beautifully colored prints of Japanese women in flamboyant native costumes. Japanese scenery or flower arrangements would be equally suitable. A variety of notepaper of this kind is available in most oriental shops at nominal prices.

ORIENTAL ATMOSPHERE

If you should want to simulate a Japanese table, you will find an exotic setting on the next page. Here are other possibilities:

TABLE. A low table could be made by placing a round, Extenda-top table over 3 apple boxes, placed close enough to the center so that they won't show, or 14-inch wrought-iron legs could be attached to a piece of 3- by 6-foot plywood.

CUSHIONS. Floor cushions are a great convenience for entertaining. They come in a great variety of shapes and exotic colors. Or, you might simply use the removable cushions from your furniture.

CLOTH OR MATS. Bamboo shades are available in many sizes from $1.00 up. They make appropriate table coverings for occasions such as this. Bamboo place mats are inexpensive, and now come in a riot of vivid colors.

Lacquered Japanese fans make colorful place mats.

CENTERPIECES. In fall or winter, use an arrangement of chrysanthemums in an oriental bowl.

In spring or summer, use an arrangement of blossoming branches such as forsythia, apple, cherry, dogwood; or ten or twelve miniature paper umbrellas scattered down the center of the table. Suspend a Japanese lantern (the white ones are lovely), from an overhead light fixture, just a little above the table. Japanese lanterns could be hung in other parts of the house as well.

Floating candles in a low bowl. (See "How-to" section.)

CHINA. Dime-store willow china would be lovely on a solid blue cloth which you could make for pennies out of yard goods. Just buy the plates, cups and saucers, and small bowls.

Here, too, you can find very small bowls of glass or pottery for mustard sauce and salad dressing.

Chopsticks and oriental soup spoons of porcelain (flat on the bottom) are easily obtainable and inexpensive.

In the entrance hall you might have a tall vase of flowering branches; on a side table, a flower arrangement made in a coolie hat.

Japanese Sukiyaki Dinner

MATS   Pearl-gray plastic with a delicate flower design

NAPKINS   Gray linen

CHINA   Flintridge, Black Contessa (white center with bands of silver and charcoal)

CENTERPIECE   Blue iris in an antique Japanese bowl

CANDLES   Black, in antique Japanese candlesticks

MISCELLANEOUS   Black iron teapot on trivet. Chopsticks on bamboo rests. Black lacquered bowls. Charcoal floor cushions. Hanging Japanese lantern.

Photo by Syzdek; table setting by B. Altman & Co.

HOW TO SERVE

Among the charms of this meal is the leisurely way it is cooked and eaten, and its informality, as it is cooked and served from the same pot.

When all your ingredients are on the table and you are ready to start the cooking, call your guests. The actual cooking before the company should be considered part of the entertainment, so do it in as leisurely a manner as possible. Act soignée about the whole thing, as if you did it every day of your life. Practice it on the family first, and you'll see how *very* simple it is. Just remember that you can't go wrong.

First the butterfly shrimp is cooked and served, one shrimp at a time to each diner. If you serve this way, each shrimp will be fresh and hot.

Then cook the Sukiyaki. When it is ready, either serve your guests, or invite them to serve themselves from the skillet in which it has been cooked. What a luscious fragrance!

Rice is passed in a bowl. Salad is served either before or after the main dish.

Invite your guests to go back for "seconds." When the main course is finished, remove the used dishes.

Dessert is served at the table from a large bowl into sherbet glasses or sauce dishes.

Tea should be served throughout the meal.

CHECK-OFF LIST FOR SEATED DINNER

Matchstick bamboo window shade or cloth or mats
Centerpiece
Candles
Napkins
Plates
Small bowls
Forks and spoons or chopsticks
Water glasses
Salt and pepper shakers
Serving forks and spoons
Serving dishes
Cigarette urns, trays, and matches
Cups and saucers
Place cards (optional); these could be propped up against crossed chopsticks in front of each plate.

"HOW-TO" SECTION

TO MAKE FLOATING CANDLES

You will need

A supply of candle ends
A large skillet half filled with water
Clean, dry cans for melting the candles
Small gelatin molds of various shapes

Directions

Simmer water in the skillet.

Place the cans holding the candle ends in the water. Keep the water at the simmer stage. *Do not allow to boil dry.*

In the meantime, cover your kitchen table

with several thicknesses of newspapers.

When the wax is melted, you remove the wicks, wipe with a paper towel, and cut into 1½-inch lengths.

Pour the candle wax into the molds. When almost hard, make a hole in the center with an ice pick and set the wick in the hole. Pour a little more melted wax into the mold. (You'll notice that as the wax hardens, the center caves in a little. That's why you usually have to add more.) Hold the wick in an upright position for a few moments until it is firm. Let the candle harden for several hours before using.

Float candles in a wide low bowl, with a few flowers floating here and there. The candles will burn for a surprisingly long time.

New england clambake

Shortly after we arrived in Newport, Rhode Island, we were invited to a genuine New England Clambake. It was held down on the rocks, overlooking the ocean on one side and the bay on the other, and we arrived just at sunset. It was a marvellous and unforgettable party. There must have been close to a hundred guests, so you can see why a professional bakemaster and assistants were needed. Preparations for a clambake are fairly extensive.

A large pit is dug usually about twenty-four hours before the party, and is lined with large rocks. A fierce driftwood fire is kept going all the night before so that the rocks will be red-hot; this is what takes so much time.

In the meantime, steaming clams are washed, sweet and white potatoes scrubbed, fish and sausage wrapped together in parchment paper, and corn on the cob and lobsters are prepared.

About an hour and a half before the Clambake is to be served, great quantities of wet seaweed are thrown on the hot rocks. The food is then added in layers. Then the whole thing is sealed tightly, and this luscious feast steams and gurgles in its own juices. You can imagine the excitement when this master-piece is unveiled and guests line up to be served.

It impressed us very much, as it is such a wonderfully different way to entertain.

Although this is far too elaborate an opera-tion for most of us, a very pleasant Clambake on a more modest scale can be served in your own dining room or outside on the ter-race. It's delicious and really a lot of fun.

Menu

Cocktails and Snacks

* *Steamed Clams, or*

* *New England Clam Chowder*

* *Steamed Lobsters*

* *Steamed Sweet Potatoes*

* *Steamed Corn on the Cob*

Cole Slaw   Cornbread Sticks

Iced Watermelon   Coffee

* *Starred items will be found in recipe section.*

When watermelon is out of season, I use layers of orange, lemon, and lime sherbet in parfait glasses for the dessert course.

If you are not able to get lobsters and fresh clams in your community, use lobster tails, available now in most frozen food de-partments of your grocery store, and substi-tute clam chowder for the steamed clams.

RECIPES

NEW ENGLAND CLAM CHOWDER
For 10

½ lb. bacon, sliced and fried crisp. Crumble up fine.
2 large potatoes, diced and browned
1 large onion, diced and browned
2 cups water. Simmer together until pota-toes are done.
Add 3 cans minced clams

1½ qts. milk
¼ lb. butter
Salt and pepper to taste.
Have in readiness 2 cups cracker crumbs.
Heat, but do not boil. Set aside for a while to ensure full flavor. At dinnertime, heat again and just before serving add the cracker crumbs. This thickens the chowder just enough, and adds a delicious flavor.

NEW ENGLAND CLAMBAKE

You will need per person:

1 pint steaming clams
1 1-lb. live lobster
2 ears corn
1 medium sweet potato

Preliminary preparations

A.M. Scrub the clams, set back in refrigerator.

Boil lobster 15 minutes. Cool, then remove tail and claws. Set back in refrigerator. (I do not use the body, as it has very little meat on it and takes up too much space in the roaster.)

Remove husks from corn, and scrub with vegetable brush to remove silk.

Scrub potatoes. Leave jackets on.

One hour before serving time

Set your electric roaster on buffet or serving table in dining room or on terrace. Set dial at 450 degrees. (For same results, use covered roasting pan in 350-degree oven.) Add 2 cups water.

Arrange potatoes on rack just above water.

One half hour before serving

Arrange layer of corn on top of potatoes.

Arrange lobster on top of corn.

Pour in the clams to fill roaster. The lid must fit snugly so that the food will steam.

❡ *The average roaster will cook enough for ten people at one time.*

The Bake is ready when the clams have opened up wide. Call your guests to the dining room, and then hear their cries of delight as the top is lifted from the roaster. It's as pretty as a painting.

SHOPPING LISTS

* Grocery List

For 10

5 qts. steaming clams
10 1-lb. live lobsters
20 ears corn
10 med. sweet potatoes
2 large heads cabbage
2 pkg. corn muffin mix
1 lb. butter
1 lb. margarine
Watermelon or 1 qt. each of lemon, orange, lime sherbet
* *Does not include staples.*

Miscellaneous list

cigarettes	equipment for game
candles	inexpensive prizes
cocktail napkins	for game
place cards	

CLAMBAKE TABLE SETTING

Although guests serve themselves buffet style, this is a sit-down dinner. On the table we use an aqua cloth covered with a fishnet; cork floats are attached to the edges of the net. Cork floats in a larger size are used as candleholders (the center hole is exactly the right size). At each place is a folded bibkin. It is shaped like a bib, but cut long so that it doubles as a napkin. Bibkins are made of dark brown Indianhead. Paper ones are now available too. In addition, plenty of paper napkins—the thick soft kind—are a must for this party.

The pottery is called "Country Fair," and is a combination of aqua and dark brown. We use plates, a large pitcher, individual melted-butter servers, square casseroles to be used as finger bowls, shell-shaped bone dishes, and salts and peppers.

For a centerpiece we place an old boat model on its side surrounded by coral candles of various lengths in the cork float holders.

Scallop shells are ideal for cigarettes and ashtrays. Lobster crackers and picks are convenient.

HOW TO SERVE

Food is set out on a long buffet, shelf, or serving table, and guests serve themselves buffet-style: first the clams, back for seconds, then the lobster and other goodies. Melted-butter containers at each place work overtime as everything—clams, lobster, potatoes, corn, cornsticks—is dunked into them. (Oh well, start on your diet *next* Monday.) Finger bowls are a must too. As you can see, this is a very informal party, and many foods here have to be eaten with the fingers.

PARTY MAID

Here's hoping you can have a party maid for this particular party. She can be a great help if she:

Refills melted-butter dishes if necessary

Keeps bone dishes emptied

Takes hot cornsticks from oven and passes them

Refills water glasses

Removes used dishes

Serves dessert

Brings coffee tray to hostess either at the table or in living room

Passes cigarettes

Keeps ashtrays emptied

Photo by Syzdek; table setting by B. Altman & Co.

New England
Clambake

CLOTH Aqua linen, topped by a fishnet with cork floats attached
NAPKINS Your choice of dark-brown linen napkins or brown Indianhead bibkins
CHINA Country Fair pottery by Carbona, a combination of aqua and brown. Seen here are plates, a pitcher, individual melted-butter servers, square casseroles to be used for finger bowls, shell bone dishes, salt and pepper set.
SILVER Stainless steel by Gentry, English Tip pattern
GLASSWARE Clear glasses with handle called "The Beer"
CENTERPIECE An old boat model half lying on its side, surrounded by coral candles of various lengths in cork float holders
MISCELLANEOUS Lobster crackers and picks. Scallop shells hold cigarettes.

HOW TO ORGANIZE

Here's a game that's fun to play, doesn't take too long, and gets the party off to a good start. You will need:

6 or 7 gaily wrapped prizes in a basket
1 pair dice, preferably the jumbo size

This game is best played sitting in a circle on the floor. Each player takes his turn throwing the dice. The object is to get two of a kind, two fours, two sixes, etc. When a player succeeds in doing this, he gets his choice of the prizes in the basket, but is not to open it.

When all the prizes are gone, the game speeds up considerably. An alarm clock is set to go off in five minutes. Game proceeds as before except those who roll two of a kind are permitted to take a prize away from any other player. The faster the game, the greater the opportunity to win someone's prize from him. When the alarm rings the game is over, and players open and keep the prize or prizes in their possession.

Ideas for prizes

Self-winding spaghetti fork
Pair of false eyelashes
Life-size pin-ups
Foxtail for car (hope an elderly person gets this)
Funny hats or caps or any other novelty you can find

Huge diamond stickpin
Mink tie
Glorified beer can opener
(I've seen even very sophisticated people play this game as if their very lives depended on it. There'll be shrieks of *"Hurry up, hurry up!* before the time runs out." You'll see—it really is fun.)

PARTY GAME

Two or three weeks ahead

Consult with your husband about your guest list, menu, other plans.

If you are going to have help with your party, engage your sitter, cateress, bartender.

Invite guests.

Several days ahead

Shop for groceries and miscellaneous items.

Check clothing you and your husband will wear.

Make up everything possible ahead of time such as salad dressing, frozen dessert, etc.

Check your table linen. Press if necessary.

Polish silver, china, glassware.

Do you need to borrow anything?

The day before

Clean house.

Wrap prizes and assemble equipment for games.

Get out your serving dishes and serving forks and spoons.

Set your table if possible and cover with cloth to protect it.

Plan on having candles somewhere in the living room as well as the dining room.

Jobs for your best beau

If cocktails are being served ask him to check supplies.

Set up a small bar on a table in living room or nearby. (For small informal parties, a sign saying SELF-SERVICE BAR is a great help to the host.)

Order or make additional ice cubes.

An open fireplace cleaned out and ready to go is a joy. Check supply of firewood.

CHECK-OFF LIST FOR SEATED DINNER

Cloth or mats
Centerpiece
Candles, approximately one per person
Plates
Flat silver
Napkins
Water glasses
Place cards
Salt and pepper shakers
Cigarette urns, matches, trays
Tray on side table with cups, saucers, spoons, cream, sugar
Melted-butter cups
Finger bowls
Bone dishes
Scissors
Nutcrackers
Oyster forks

SCHEDULE FOR PARTY DAY

A.M. Prepare salad ingredients and store in refrigerator.

Put fresh cigarettes in containers.

Set out additional ashtrays, lighters, coasters.

Select phonograph records.

Arrange centerpiece for table.

Tack up menu in convenient location.

Make list of jobs for party maid if any.

P.M. Rest for an hour or two if possible.

4:30 Dress.

5:30 Inspect the bathroom. Set out clean towels, cleansing tissues, fresh soap, extra bathroom tissue, face powder and individual puffs, individual lipsticks in several shades.

5:45 Light fire in fireplace.

6:00 Put on porch light.

Set out snack tray.

6:15 Start record player—gay, light music —playing softly.

Light candles in living room; use lamplight, not strong overhead lights.

6:30 Guests start arriving. Direct them to the room set aside for their coats. Make introductions.

As soon as guests are seated, offer them cigarettes, and cocktails if you are serving cocktails. Otherwise ginger ale or fruit juice is always acceptable. The main thing is, offer them *something*. It serves to dispel the formality that sometimes exists early in a party.

6:30 Start electric roaster. Potatoes only at first.

7:00 Add the corn, lobsters, clams.

Pop the cornsticks into the oven.

Make coffee.

7:15 Set out cream, ice water, melted butter, and salad.

7:30 Light candles and call your guests to dinner.

After dinner serve coffee and liqueurs in the living room, followed by games or singing. Flash pictures of the party are fun to have as souvenirs.

Congratulations! Your party was a great success.

Shishkebab fireside supper

The wind is moaning mournfully, snow and sleet are hissing against the windowpanes, and you dream longingly of summertime and barbecues on the lawn.

Don't let it get you down. Defeat the elements and plan a Shishkebab Fireside Supper.

Your guests will develop a hearty appetite listening to the kebabs sizzling on the grate and watching them come to a nice toasty brown right in your living-room fireplace.

A long-playing record of haunting gypsy-violin melodies will add to the romantic atmosphere.

EQUIPMENT

Compact, efficient, portable barbecues are available for as little as $2.50, and will fit right inside your fireplace. I believe you'll get years of service out of one of these, and it will come in handy later on as an auxiliary barbecue when you're entertaining a large group. In addition such grills are collapsible and are easy to pack, so it is convenient to take one on an outing.

You will also need steel skewers—about 12 to 15 inches long; you should have one for each guest. Most houseware departments have them at prices ranging from 25 to 95 cents apiece, depending on quality and length.

Menu

* Barbecued Shishkebabs

* Pilaf with Pine Nuts

* Red Cabbage–Apple Casserole

Celery, Carrot Stocks, Green Onions

Baklava or * Bint Assahn

* Flaming Coffee

* Starred items will be found in the recipe section.

TABLE AND SERVICE

I suggest that you keep these aspects of the party as informal as possible.

I usually assemble in one place the equipment I will need, and set the tables just a few moments before serving time.

I use a 54- by 72-inch cloth over two card tables pushed together, providing comfortable seating accommodations for six guests. If possible, set up the tables in the same room in which you are barbecuing the kebabs. In this way, diners can reheat their kebabs if they wish. (I told you it was a very informal party.)

RECIPES FOR 6

BARBECUED SHISHKEBABS

You will need:

Leg of lamb, 5–6 lb. cut into 1½-inch cubes
Sauce for marinating
12 small firm tomatoes
12 small onions, parboiled
18 1½-inch squares of green pepper

Sauce for marinating

¾ cup olive oil
¾ cup wine or sherry (Burgundy is especially
  good)
1 crushed clove garlic
2 small minced onions

1 tsp. dry mustard
1 tbsp. Worcestershire sauce
2 tsp. salt
1 tsp. fresh ground pepper
1 tsp. oregano
½ tsp. marjoram
½ tsp. Accent

CHECK-OFF LIST FOR TABLE

Cloth
Paper napkins
Silver
Plates (heated,
  please)
Water glasses

Salts and peppers
Serving forks
  and spoons
Cigarette trays
  and matches
Candles (optional)

Cups and saucers and cream and sugar could
be brought in later with dessert.

SUPPER'S READY

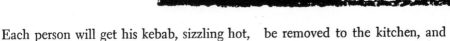

Each person will get his kebab, sizzling hot, from the chef.

Pilaf and cabbage in casseroles will be placed on the table and passed, family style.

When main course is finished, plates will be removed to the kitchen, and the dessert served individually on a butter or salad plate.

Coffee will be served by the hostess assisted by the host.

The night before the party. Make the marinade sauce, and place cubes of lamb in it, being sure that all pieces are being marinated. The next day turn the meat in the sauce a few times.

Several hours before the party. Place the meat cubes alternately on skewers with the tomatoes, mushrooms, green peppers, and parboiled onions. Arrange on platter and refrigerate until ready.

In the meantime, set up your grill in the fireplace and build a deep fire of charcoal briquets. Allow about 45 minutes for fire to burn down to the desired, glowing-coals stage; some white ashes should show.

Bring out the platter of kebabs to be admired, then have the chef gently lay them on the grill. They should be cooked about 3 inches from the coals. Allow about 25 minutes' cooking time. *Serve while hot.* (Kebabs can be broiled in the oven.)

PILAF

1 tbsp. butter or margarine
1 onion, minced
3 cups Minute Rice
2 cans consommé or chicken broth
2 cans water
1 bottle pine nuts or 1 cup slivered blanched almonds

Brown onion in butter.
Add dry rice and brown.
Add rice and onion to rapidly boiling water and consommé.
Turn off heat. Add the nuts.
Cover and let stand 15 to 20 minutes, until water is absorbed and each grain of rice is separate. Transfer to buttered casserole, and keep in oven with soft cloth over it so that it will remain warm and fluffy until ready to serve.

RED CABBAGE AND APPLE CASSEROLE

1 head red cabbage, shredded
6 tart apples, pared, cored, and sliced
¾ cup boiling water
1½ tsp. salt
¼ tsp. fresh ground pepper
¼ cup sherry or wine vinegar
1 tsp. cornstarch
2 tbsp. melted butter
1 tbsp. grape jelly (optional)
¼ cup brown sugar
Butter to dot top

Cook cabbage for 10 minutes in boiling water.
Add apples. Cook for 10 minutes more with pan covered.
Make a paste of the salt, pepper, vinegar, cornstarch, melted butter, and grape jelly. Add to cabbage and apples and mix well.
Place in casserole, sprinkle with the brown sugar, and dot with butter. Reheat in oven, about 20 minutes at 350 degrees.

* BINT ASSAHN

Pastry with honey

¼ lb. butter
2¼ cups all-purpose flour
½ tsp. salt
3 eggs
½ cup milk
½ cup chopped nuts
¼ cup melted butter
Honey

Work butter into flour. Add salt. Beat eggs and add the eggs and milk to the flour and mix well. Divide the dough into small balls

about the size of an egg. Work each ball into a very flat, wafer-thin circle like a pizza. The size of the pastry depends on the skill of the cook in flattening out the round balls of dough. A skillful cook aims for wafer-thin layers of dough which produce a flat, circular pastry after cooking. Place a circle on a round pie tin or on a cookie sheet, spread with melted butter, and sprinkle with finely chopped nuts. Lay another circle lightly on the first, spread with butter and sprinkle with nuts. Continue until all the circles form one stack. Bake about 45 minutes in a 350-degree oven or until golden brown. Serve hot with more butter and honey. Yield: six servings.

* *From* Favorite Recipes from the United Nations, *published by the U.S. Committee for the United Nations.*

FLAMING COFFEE

You will need:

Coffee
Cognac

Small cognac spoons which hook over cup (50 cents each, available from Hennessey, P.O. Box 34 A, Mt. Vernon, New York).

Fill coffee cups.

Hook spoon over the top, and pour cognac into spoon to warm.

Ignite. Leave in spoon for a moment, then float the flaming cognac on top of the coffee. Delicious, and very pretty in a darkened room.

GROCERY LIST *

Leg of lamb	Consommé or
Tomatoes	chicken broth
Small onions	Pine nuts or almonds
Green pepper	Red cabbage
Olive oil	Apples
Celery	† Baklava
Carrots	Cognac
Green onions	Sherry or other red
Minute Rice	wine

* Does not include staples.

† Baklava is a delicious and unusual pastry of Near East origin. It can be ordered from the Liberty Oriental Pastry Co., 281 Audubon Ave., New York City, N.Y. They will ship anywhere in the United States, postpaid.

Chinese chow supper

ORIENTAL ATMOSPHERE

Lighted Chinese lanterns, bright as butterflies, the fragrance of sandalwood from a burning joss stick, Chinese wind chimes tinkling gaily in the doorways, and the host and hostess resplendent in oriental robes set the stage for a Chinese Chow party, and you can be sure that you and your guests will have a wonderful time.

As so many of our friends in service life have acquired Japanese or Chinese costumes, we usually ask guests to wear costume if they wish, but that is a decision that is up to the hostess.

An inexpensive favor which we give to each guest as he comes in is a fascinating 14-inch-long cigarette holder. It resembles an opium pipe. The cigarette fits in the end in a vertical position. Even non-smokers will want to experiment with this. They are available in most Chinese stores, and sometimes even in the ten-cent store.

Almost everyone likes Chinese food. However, on my written invitation, I always specify "Chinese Chow," in case any of the invited guests don't care for it.

Menu

Lobster Egg Foo Yung on Noodles

Almond Chicken, Fluffy Rice

Barbecued Pork Cubes on Skewers

Cinnamon Apples

Iced Watermelon Pickles

Mandarin Salad

Chinese Fortune Cakes

Food for the Gods   Tea

Candied Ginger

Starred items will be found in the recipe section.

RECIPES FOR 8

LOBSTER EGG FOO YUNG

1 cup onions, chopped, browned
1 cup bamboo shoots, cut into threads 2 inches long
2 small cans water chestnuts, chopped fine
1 can bean sprouts, well drained
1 tbsp. salt
½ tsp. pepper
1½ cups lobster, fresh, frozen or canned, chopped fine
16 eggs, well beaten

Combine ingredients and mix well. Melt ¼ lb. margarine in heavy skillet. Drop egg mixture, about 1 tbsp. for each patty into heated fat. Cook slowly on both sides until firm. (Three or four patties can be made at one time.) Place the cooked patties, or Chinese pancakes as they are sometimes called, into medium thin gravy, preferably pork or chicken, which has been heating in the top of a double boiler or chafing dish. Sprinkle soy sauce over gravy sparingly. As each new egg patty is added, baste with the gravy. Serve piping hot over crisp noodles.

ALMOND CHICKEN

1. Marinate 2 cups cubed chicken in 4 tbsp. soy sauce, 2 tbsp. cornstarch and 4 tbsp. sherry.
2. Brown 1 cup celery, ½ cup onion, 1 cup mushrooms.
3. Add 10 diced water chestnuts, 1 cup bamboo shoots, 2 cups salted almonds, 1 can cream of chicken soup, and the chicken mixture.
4. Heat well and serve with fluffy rice.

BARBECUED PORK CUBES ON SKEWERS

Cook one pork chop per person. Remove bone and cut meat into 1-inch cubes. Marinate in barbecue sauce * 2 hours, then string on 6-inch skewers. (I use the kind found in household departments for securing the neck opening in turkey.) Brown under broiler.

◖ *These taste something like barbecued spare ribs, but are meatier.*

MANDARIN SALAD

Chunks of lettuce served with homemade boiled dressing and finely chopped blanched almonds.

FOOD FOR THE GODS
(*and it really is*)

Blend together ¼ lb. margarine, 1 tbsp. sugar, 1 cup flour. Place in cake pan and press down with your fingers so that it lines the bottom evenly. Bake 15 min. 350°. It must not be too brown. Cool. In the meantime mix together 2 eggs, 1 cup brown sugar, 1 tbsp. flour, 1 tsp. vanilla, 1 cup chopped walnuts, ½ cup cocoanut. Pour on top of cooled pastry. Bake at 275 degrees until set, and ice while warm. Use a thin icing made by combining 1 cup confectioner's sugar with a very small amount of water, and 1 tsp. lemon or vanilla flavoring. To serve cut in small squares.

SHOPPING LISTS

Grocery list

Lobster	Cinnamon apples
Eggs	Watermelon pickles
Water chestnuts	Lettuce
Bean sprouts	Candied ginger
Bamboo shoots	Onions
Chicken	Mushrooms

Noodles	Salted almonds
Rice	Walnuts
Pork chops	Cocoanut
Soy sauce	

Miscellaneous list

Cigarettes	Cocktail napkins
Flowers	Place cards
Candles	Favors if desired

CHINESE CHOW TABLE

An exceptionally pretty table can be achieved by combining oriental dinnerware with modern accessories.

Here we have used black straw oval-shaped place mats as a background for the exotic chinaware in a heavenly blue-green, with shades of pink and lilac in the pattern. As a contrast we used pink linen napkins.

The bamboo-handled silverware further carries out the Far East look, as do chopsticks shooting out from a brass container.

As a centerpiece, lilac-colored chrysanthemum pompons are arranged simply in a brass bowl flanked by a pair of smaller square bowls in which tiny blossoms and flower candles float on the surface.

Photo by Syzdek; table setting by B. Altman & Co.

Chinese
Chow
Supper

TABLE MATS Black straw, oval shaped

NAPKINS Pink linen

CHINA Hong Kong import (bluish-green background, shades of pink and lilac in the pattern)

SILVER Bamboo-handled ware

CENTERPIECE Brass bowl with simple arrangement of lilac-colored chrysanthemum pompons, flanked by a pair of smaller bowls in which tiny blossoms and flower candles are floating

MISCELLANEOUS Chopsticks shoot out of the brass container at the left

ALTERNATE BUDGET SETTING

An alternate setting for the budget-minded which is, in its way, just as effective has as its background a vivid blue tablecloth or table mats.

For plates you can use the small octagonal white platters which may be found at most variety stores for about 29 cents each. These are slightly larger than conventional dinner plates, and well suited for a Chinese dinner with its many dishes and condiments.

Inexpensive dark blue goblets give a brilliant bit of color, as do blue candles. I use the bottom sections of a pair of hurricane lamps which are of white metal. The bases have an upturned rim in which I arrange small blue and white flowers. (Any white candlesticks would be pretty.) Blue bachelor buttons and white daisies or pompons are particularly good, and may be placed around the base of the candlesticks.

If you have any white Chinese figures, group them as a centerpiece with blue glass chips sprinkled at random around them.*

It is fun to place chopsticks at each place. Many people are able to eat with them very well and are justly proud of the accomplishment. But I take pity on the others, including myself, and provide forks.

Place small pitchers of soy sauce here and there.

These glass chips, sparkling like jewels, give life to the whole table. Aquarium stores usually have them, and I've seen them often in department stores. They are inexpensive and come in a wide assortment of colors.

SERVICE

Cocktails will be served beforehand in the living room or library.

Lobster Egg Foo Yung can be prepared in the kitchen and kept hot in a chafing dish.

The Almond Chicken and Barbecued Pork Cubes should all be kept hot either in chafing dishes, over a candle burner, or on one of the new electric trivets. If you bake your rice, serve it in the same casserole to avoid chilling. Chinese food *must* be served hot to be good. Have you noticed that restaurants usually use covered casseroles for serving?

The egg foo yung cakes may be cooked at the table in an electric frying pan by the hostess, or she may assign this task to one of her guests. When finished, they are placed in the hot gravy in the chafing dish. When the cakes are made this way, they are light as a feather, and the procedure also adds a little extra atmosphere to the party.

Inasmuch as this is a very informal affair, the food could be placed on the table and passed family style. It would be well to have two teapots, one at each end, to keep everyone supplied. If you wish you might have coffee on hand too for those who prefer it.

When the main course is finished, the table is cleared with the exception of the centerpiece and water glasses.

Then dessert plates are brought in and the dessert and the candied ginger (which has been cut in shoestring strips) are passed.

YOUR FUTURE

This is a good time to bring out the Chinese Fortunetelling Game, obtainable in many oriental shops.

This is a round cardboard box, filled with sticks resembling tongue depressors. Each one is numbered. The box is passed around the table, and each guest carefully shakes out one stick. This is the key to his fortune, which is given in an accompanying book under his number. The fortune is referred to and read aloud. Some of these are hilarious, and you may be sure that everyone is anxious to hear his fortune.

HOW TO ORGANIZE

Two or three weeks ahead

Consult with your husband on your guest list, menu, and other plans.
If you are going to have help with your party, engage your sitter, cateress, bartender.
Invite guests.

Several days ahead

Shop for groceries and miscellaneous items.
Check clothing you and your husband intend to wear.
If you have a freezer, you can make these things in advance and freeze:

> Lobster egg foo yung, with the exception of eggs

> Almond chicken
> Barbecued pork kabobs
> Food for the Gods

Make your boiled dressing for salad.
Check your linen; press if necessary.
Polish silver, china, glassware.
Do you need to borrow anything?

The day before

Clean house.
Set your table if possible.
Get out serving dishes and forks and spoons.
Plan on having candles in the living room as well as on the table.
Prepare food and store in refrigerator overnight.

CHECK-OFF LIST FOR TABLE SETTING
Tablecloth or mats
Centerpiece
Candles
Plates
Flat silver and chopsticks
Napkins
Water glasses
Place cards
Salt and pepper shakers
Cigarette urns, trays, matches
Tray on side table with cups, saucers, teapots

Jobs for your best beau

If cocktails are being served, ask him to check supplies.

Set up a small bar on a table in living room or somewhere nearby. (For small, informal parties, a sign saying SELF-SERVICE BAR is a great help to the host.)

Order or make ice cubes the day before.

If fireplace is to be used see that it is cleaned out and ready for fire.

SCHEDULE FOR PARTY DAY

A.M. Prepare salad ingredients and store in refrigerator.

Put fresh cigarettes in containers.

Set out additional ashtrays, lighters, coasters.

Select phonograph records.

Tack up menu in convenient location.

Make list of jobs for cateress if any.

Remove frozen foods from freezer.

P.M. Rest for an hour or two if possible.

5:00 Dress.

6:00 Inspect the bathroom. Set out Kleenex, fresh soap, extra bathroom tissue, face powder, individual lipsticks in several colors.

6:15 Light fire in fireplace.

6:30 Porch light on.

Set out snack tray.

6:45 Start record player. Gay, light music, playing softly.

Light candles in living room. Have lamplight, no strong overhead lights.

7:00 Guests start arriving. Direct them to the room set aside for their coats. As soon as they are introduced around and seated, offer them cocktails.

7:15 Start heating your main dishes in oven or double boiler.

7:45 Set out cream, ice water; mix salad and set on table with salad fork and spoon.

Heat barbecued pork cubes under broiler turned low.

8:00 Make tea, and make plenty.

Set food on table. Have you taken everything from refrigerator?

Light candles and call your guests to "chow."

Happy eating!

Snapshots of this party are fun to have, especially the kind made with a Land Camera, which develops the picture in 60 seconds.

One further suggestion. An alternative to cooking these foods yourself is to order them in advance from a Chinese restaurant, and have them delivered or picked up just at dinnertime. Set the scene for the party as if you were cooking yourself.

Easter brunch

Easter is a day of many delights—the family procession to church on a Spring morning, with the green leaves bursting forth; the expectant hush in tiny chapels and great cathedrals alike; and the solemnity and joy of the Easter service.

Yes, it is a day dear to the hearts of all, a family day, a day for children. Make them happy by including them in your plans.

Laura and Bill usually plan an Easter Brunch after church. They've found it a pleasant way to entertain family and friends, and children are always included in the invitation.

This party is planned so that Laura will have a minimum of last-minute preparation. She prepares everything the day before. Even the table is set ahead of time. In this way she can attend church with the others, serene in the knowledge that everything is in readiness, and all that remains to be done is the heating of the food.

APPROXIMATE SCHEDULE

1:00   Guests assemble
1:00–1:30 Egg nog for adults
          Children open and play with their
          Easter Basket surprise presents
          in another room

1:30–2:30 Brunch is served
2:30–4:30 Easter Parade, or
        Egg Hunt and other games for
        children

FESTIVE ATMOSPHERE

We happily received an invitation to this party last year, and will always treasure the memory of it. The host's home was gaily bedecked for the occasion. As we walked up the path, we noticed how pretty the pots of blue hyacinths looked in the windows framed by snowy white criss-cross curtains. As we were lovingly received and our wraps disposed of, we were entranced by the heavenly fragrance from the Easter lilies and hyacinths.

SEE WHAT THE BUNNY BROUGHT

After greetings had been exchanged and Easter outfits admired, Laura produced a very happy surprise for the children. Each one was presented with an Easter Basket, but instead of being filled with candy, it was filled with little gifts such as might be found in a Christmas stocking, each one attractively wrapped (see How-to section).

The baskets, as you can imagine, were received with joyful enthusiasm, and the children, led by their young host Tommy, repaired to the playroom to open and admire their gifts.

In the meantime the adults were served egg nogs which they enjoyed while sitting around the flickering fire.

TURQUOISE AND LILAC TABLE

In a surprisingly short time, Laura called us to the dining room for brunch.

What a picture! The table was done in various shades of turquoise and lilac—perfect Easter colors. The tablecloth was of turquoise linen with lilac napkins providing a striking contrast. The chinaware, called "Spring Garden," had sprays of violets in various shades of lavender and purple against a white background.

The eye-catching centerpiece delighted both adults and children. It was an Easter bonnet * tree. Bare branches had been secured on a pinpoint holder in a wicker basket which was then filled with colored Easter eggs and tiny sprigs of flowers. Jelly beans were sprinkled on the cloth around the basket. Miniature Easter bonnets in various colors had been hung on the branches. In addition to the "tree," a miniature hat box and hat were set on the table above each place setting.

On the opposite page is a photograph of this delightful table.

The bonnets are doll hats, available in variety stores. They were redecorated with velvet ribbon and flowers.

Photo by Syzdek; table setting by B. Altman & Co.

Easter Brunch

CLOTH   Turquoise linen

NAPKINS   Lilac linen

CHINA   Noritake's Spring Garden (shades of lavender and purple on white)

SILVER   Fontana by Towle

GLASSWARE   Oxford by Heisey

CENTERPIECE   Miniature Easter bonnets suspended from the tips of branches secured in wicker basket. (These are doll hats re-decorated with velvet ribbons and flowers. Face-powder boxes have been beribboned and be-flowered to resemble hat boxes.) Various shades of Easter eggs are arranged in the basket, and jelly beans for the children are sprinkled around the base.

THREE ALTERNATE IDEAS FOR EASTER ARRANGEMENTS

Branches sprayed green can be secured in flower pot; suspend decorated, blown-out Easter eggs, bows, and tiny bunches of flowers from the branches. To hang the decorations, you'll find Christmas ornament hangers convenient.

Do you have an outmoded Easter bonnet, preferably a generously beribboned one? If so, use it as a flower container. Cut small holes here and there in the crown. Lay it in the center of the table over a bowl of water. Insert stems of fresh flowers through the holes so that the flowers look like trimming on the hat.

Spray an old birdcage to match your color scheme. Arrange a bouquet of fresh flowers and vines so that they cascade out the top and sides.

Delicious Brunch Food

* Egg Nog

* Grapefruit Baskets

(filled with grapefruit sections and grapes)

* Chicken Livers and Mushrooms
on Toast Points

* Western Scrambled Eggs

Ready-Mix Blueberry Muffins

Hot Cross Buns

Coffee   Strawberry Milk

* Starred items will be found in recipe section.

SERVICE

Egg Nog was served in the living room before brunch.

Grapefruit baskets were in place on the table.

Chicken livers and mushrooms were kept hot in a chafing dish. Scrambled eggs were kept hot over a candle warmer. These were set on a shelf which ran the full width of the dining room. It was 18 inches wide, and wonderfully convenient for serving buffet meals. Guests were invited to serve themselves. In the meantime the grapefruit course was removed.

Muffins and hot cross buns were kept hot in the oven, then passed at the table after guests were reseated.

Coffee was poured at the table.

Strawberry milk was at each child's place.

GAMES FOR CHILDREN

EASTER EGG HUNT

Preliminary preparations. Dye eggs in the same colors that you have used to decorate the Easter baskets (four or five of each color should be enough). Hide the eggs all over the house or yard.

To play. Explain to each child that he is to gather only the eggs that match the ribbon on his basket. For example, if he has a yellow ribbon, he gathers all the yellow eggs. Children take home the eggs they find.

RABBIT RACE

Mark off a start and finish line.

Children place their heels together. At the word "go," they jump rather than run toward the finish line. Heels must be kept together (harder than you'd think!) during the race.

Award a prize to the winning rabbit.

FIND THE EASTER BUNNY

Name one of the children to be the Easter Bunny. He hides while the children count to fifty. Then they all start to look for him. When a player does find him, he keeps quiet about it, and hides along with him. And so it goes until all the players find the Easter Bunny. Last one to find him is Easter Bunny next time.

BUNNY NEST

Fill a small jar or basket with candy Easter eggs and have a guessing contest as to how many eggs in the basket. The guesses of all the children are marked down. The basket or jar of Easter candy goes to the contestant whose guess was most nearly accurate.

"HOW-TO" SECTION

EASTER EGG PLACE CARDS

Wash and dry the eggs carefully.

Write guests' names with wax crayons, then dip in egg dye. (The name will remain uncolored.) Decorate with sequins or glitter.

Place
on fold

Place
on fold

Jommy

Fold back here

so that card
will stand

BUNNY PLACE CARDS
Alternate

Fold a piece of colored construction paper. Place the pattern with the tops of the ears on the fold. With sharp scissors, cut out around the pattern being careful not to cut off the tops of the ears. That section will act as the hinge. Add the name and the "cottontail" with a white pencil. Fold along the dotted line. The bunny is now double and will stand up nicely on the table in front of each guest.

EASTER BASKET FAVORS
FOR CHILDREN

Buy a package of green cellophane straw and an Easter basket from the ten-cent store for each child. Tuck in four or five dime-store items.

Suggestions for the girls:

Bracelet or necklace	Doll dishes
Hairbow	Embroidery or
Plastic apron	sewing kit
Doll	Bunny balloon

Suggestions for the boys:

Bow tie	Cowboy scarf
Wallet	Modeling clay
Marbles	Balloon
Toy truck	

Wrap each present in paper of a different color. (Tissue is now available in many lovely colors.) Secure with ribbons or Easter egg seals in bright colors. Place the favors in the baskets, and decorate each one with a bow of a different color—pink, blue, green, yellow. Tuck in one or two little yellow chenille chickens. Present one to each child. These will give the children much more pleasure than too much candy.

RECIPES

EGG NOG

16 to 20 punch cup servings

10 eggs
1½ cups confectioner's sugar
1 qt. milk
1 pt. light cream
½ pt. whipping cream
½ tsp. salt
½ tsp. nutmeg
½ tsp. cinnamon
1 tsp. vanilla or rum flavoring

Beat the eggs well.

Add milk, light cream, and seasonings. Beat well. Store in refrigerator.

At serving time, pour into chilled punch-bowl, float the whipped cream on top. Serve in punch cups with a sprinkle of nutmeg or cinnamon on top.

GRAPEFRUIT BASKETS

Cut grapefruit in half.

Carefully remove the segments and juice and set aside in bowl.

Scrape the inside of the grapefruit until you have just the skin left.

To make handles:

Cut a ½-inch strip from the rim, leaving it attached at opposite sides. Lift up the strips and tie together with pastel ribbon in a bow.

Cut grapes in half, and remove the seeds. Mix with the grapefruit segments and add sugar. Store covered in refrigerator until ready to serve.

At serving time, pile the fruit into the shells.

CHICKEN LIVERS AND MUSHROOMS

in brown sauce on toast points
To serve 8

1 lb. fresh mushrooms or 2 large cans
¼ lb. margarine
1 onion
2½ lb. frozen chicken livers
1 cup flour (in which to coat the chicken livers)
2 cups left over beef or chicken gravy
1 tbsp. Kitchen Bouquet or Brown-Quick
Salt and pepper to taste

Remove stems from mushrooms. Slice mushroom caps and brown gently in margarine. Set aside.

Slice onion fine and brown. Set aside.

Drain chicken livers on paper towel, then shake in flour in paper bag. Brown gently and set aside.

Add gravy to remaining fat in the pan. Add Kitchen Bouquet. Simmer for 5 minutes, stirring constantly. Add a little water, if necessary. Should be the consistency of a medium white sauce.

Add chicken livers, mushrooms and onions to gravy. Season to taste. Keep hot in chafing dish. Serve on toast points.

SCRAMBLED EGGS, WESTERN STYLE

8 eggs
4 tbsp. minced onion
4 tbsp. minced green pepper
4 tbsp. chopped cooked ham or crisp bacon
 bits
½ cup light cream
½ tsp. Lawry's Seasoned Salt
2 tbsp. Heinz chili sauce

Combine ingredients. Set in refrigerator until ready. Beat just enough so that ingredients are well mixed. Fry slowly in butter, stirring constantly until eggs are thickened. Do not overcook.

GROCERY LIST *

Eggs for nog and brunch	Onion	Whipping cream	Blueberry muffin mix
Confectioner's sugar	Chicken livers	Grapefruit	Bakery hot cross buns
Milk	Bread	Grapes	Strawberry syrup (for
Light cream	Green pepper	Mushrooms	strawberry milk)
	Cooked ham or bacon		

* Does not include staples.

4th of July

Family picnic

The Fourth of July is a wonderful time to plan a real old-fashioned family picnic with food, games, contests, prizes, campfire, and everything. Not only will you enjoy it thoroughly yourselves, but it will provide memories that your children will cherish always.

With work and expenses divided, there'll be no strain on any one person.

This merry picnic is planned for eight couples and ten children, with an estimated cost of $1.50 per person for everything.

PLANNING YOUR PICNIC

Making plans for a picnic is one of the most enjoyable parts of it. To assure that everything will run smoothly, and to avoid the disappointment of leaving important equipment at home, it is wise to put someone in charge of each department. The most important ones will be:

Money

Grounds

Food

Table setting

Games

To keep money matters straight, appoint a banker. After the menu has been decided on, games and prizes discussed, and other expenses considered, the total cost of the picnic is estimated, the cost is divided equally among the families, and the money is paid to the banker. Most of us find it more pleasant to pay for entertainment in advance than after the fun is all over. The banker will reimburse those who purchased supplies for the party.

PICNIC SITE

Because this is such a popular holiday, it is wise to make reservations for your picnic grounds well ahead of time. Keep in mind the following conveniences:

Available drinking water;
Bathing facilities;
Shelter in case of rain;
Rest rooms;
Fireplace, or a place where it is permissible to build a fire.

PROGRAM OF THE DAY

Here is an approximate schedule for this picnic:

4 P.M. Assemble
4–5   Swimming or hiking
5–6   Games and contests
6–7   Picnic supper
      Awarding of prizes
7–8   Baseball
      Horseshoes
      Follow the leader
8–9   Campfire fun—ghost stories, tall tales, sing-song, then home

It could be scheduled earlier in the day as a picnic lunch rather than a supper. In this way the families could get home before dark. This alternate schedule would work out particularly well if there were plans to attend a fireworks display.

PICNIC MENUS

Every family has favorite traditional picnic recipes. Geographical location too has a lot to do with determining the menu. In New England it would probably be a clam and lobster bake; in the Southwest you might choose steak barbecued on a portable grill; in the South, it would probably be Southern Fried Chicken. When the Food Committee gets together, they'll no doubt come up with fine ideas. Here is my favorite picnic menu.

Favorite Picnic Menu

Fried Chicken

Thin Bread and Butter Sandwiches

Potato Salad, Homemade Boiled Dressing

Celery, Olives, Pickles, Devilled Eggs

Homemade Freezer Ice Cream

Cake

Lemonade   Hot Coffee   Milk

RED, WHITE, AND BLUE TABLE

A gaily set table adds to the enjoyment of any party. This one is planned with an eye on the budget, but is colorful and festive. We start with picnic tables and benches. Use red, white, and blue striped tablecloths made of yard goods. (Will be useful later on for any patriotic celebration.) With this we use bright blue and bright red paper napkins. Fold a red and a blue napkin together, one overlapping the other so that both colors show.

White plastic knives, forks, and spoons are available at very low prices. Tuck them into the napkin fold. Use white paper plates and mugs.

Use one of these as a centerpiece:

A cake with white fluffy frosting. If the cake is to be served after dark, insert sparklers and ignite each one just before serving. On a square white-iced cake, make diagonal stripes alternately with raspberries and blueberries for a nice red, white, and blue effect.

A cluster of red, white, and blue balloons anchored with a brick.

Shooting star candles in a row.

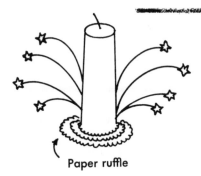

Paper ruffle

HOW TO MAKE "SHOOTING STAR" CANDLES

Buy or make fat, round candles 6 inches or more high and about 2 inches in diameter. Stick on red and blue gummed stars in assorted sizes. With cellophane tape attach fine wires 6 to 10 inches long about ½ inch above base. Arch out as in illustration. Stick small blue stars back to back on wire tips.

CHECK-OFF LIST FOR PICNIC TABLES

Cloths	Serving dishes
Napkins	Cream and sugar
Plates	Bottle and can
Mugs	openers
Forks and spoons	Centerpiece
Salt and pepper	
Serving forks and	
spoons	

GAMES AND CONTESTS

Old-fashioned games and contests are half the fun at a picnic. Here is one way to get a good selection:

Each family attending plans one event. As the crowd is assembling each family draws a number from the hat. Beginning with number one, they all participate in whatever game is suggested.

Here are some others from which to choose:

THE WHISTLE RACE
Everyone

Of all races, this is the funniest one to watch, and will get things off to a hilarious start.

Mark "Start" and "Finish" lines 100 feet apart. At the whistle, everyone races toward the Finish Line. Just as they get nicely started, the whistle blows again; now they must turn around and run the other way. Blow whistle three or four times. Each time contestants must reverse. First one over the Finish Line wins. (It could well be the smallest child.)

PEANUT SCRAMBLE
Children

Line the children up 20 feet from the man with the peanuts. At the word "go," he throws the peanuts in every direction. All the children scramble for them.

NAIL-DRIVING CONTEST
Men

Provide each contestant with a piece of lumber, a handful of 3-inch nails, and a hammer. The one who drives the greatest number of nails in a one-minute period wins. Forfeit two points for every nail driven crooked.

POTATO RACE
Couples

This will bring back memories of bygone Sunday School picnics. It's still a good race. Couples compete.

For eight couples, place two potatoes in each of eight piles about 50 feet from starting line. At the signal, Mom races to the potatoes, picks one up, and runs back to touch Dad's hand. He runs back to pick up the remaining potato and races the other men back to the finish line.

THREE-LEGGED RACE
Children

Contestants run in pairs. Try to match them evenly in height. They stand side by side, and the right ankle of one contestant is tied to the left ankle of his partner with a piece of soft cloth. At the word "go," they race three-legged to the Finish Line. (Give them a few minutes to practice first.)

SNAKE WALK
Adults

Mark "Start" and "Finish" lines 15 feet apart. At the signal, each contestant steps forward with his left foot, then swings his right foot behind the left, so that the right foot is to the left and slightly in front of the left as it touches the ground. The left foot is then swung behind the right in the same manner, and so on.

BIRDS IN THE NEST
Children

Give each child a bag containing about 30 marbles. The object of the game is to guess how many marbles an opponent has in his clenched fist. Randy goes up to Nancy and, with fist outstretched, says, "How many birds in the nest?" If Nancy guesses five, and Randy has five, she gets the marbles for herself. If, on the other hand, she guesses one, she has to forfeit the difference which is four marbles. Set a time limit.

PET RACE
Adults

You will need six dime-store stuffed animals, each one wearing a ribbon in a different color—red, green, purple, orange, yellow, blue. Make a race track, eight feet long, by laying twine or tape on the ground like this:

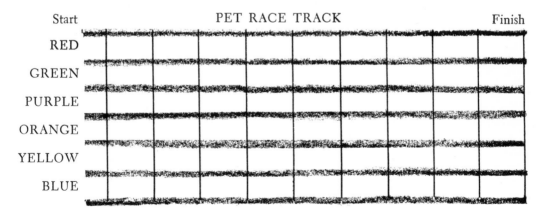

Start	PET RACE TRACK	Finish
RED		
GREEN		
PURPLE		
ORANGE		
YELLOW		
BLUE		

You will also need six slips of art paper about 1 inch square in each of the above colors. On the red slips write UP 1; UP 2; UP 3; BACK 1; BACK 2; BACK 3. Do the same with the other colors. Place all slips in a hat and shake up.

To play: Six players place entries at starting post. The leader draws a slip from the hat, and calls out "Red, move up 3," or "Blue, go back 1." Players move their pets forward or backward in the squares according to the calls.

It makes the game even more exciting if you have an announcer calling out "Purple is leading by two lengths, Yellow is second by three lengths, Blue is coming up behind," etc. First pet over the finish line wins.

First, second, and third prize ribbons. Instead of buying prizes, why not use blue, red, and white ribbons for first, second, and third prizes for each game.

Notes should be made regarding the winners of each race, then the winners of all contests are announced, and ribbons given out as you are finishing supper. Bring a supply of pins so that the trophies can be proudly displayed.

AFTER-SUPPER FUN

Take your choice of these:
>   Horseshoe contest
>   Baseball game, men versus women
>   Follow the leader

Baseball game. This will be one of the highlights of the picnic. On first thought, you may say, "But that's no contest." But— there's a catch to it! The men have to run backward to the base, and they have to catch and pitch left-handed. (Or if normally left-handed, they must pitch and catch right-handed.)

Whatever you do, include this in your plans.

Holiday open house

Some of my happiest childhood memories are those of the calls the entire family made on friends at Christmastime. We lived in Calgary, Alberta, Canada, and could pretty well count on a white Christmas each year.

What fun it was to dress up in our new holiday outfits, pile our gaily wrapped gifts in a basket, and set off to visit our nearest and dearest. Nowadays children are seldom included in invitations, and this seems particularly unfortunate at Christmas.

Last year a friend of ours, Mrs. Morey, included the whole family in invitations to her open house. Not only children, but grandmothers or other relatives living with the family were invited, and a very gay party it was—as much fun for Great-grandmother as for six-year-old Susie. The party was such an outstanding success that the Moreys plan to make it an annual affair. And we'd certainly like to be invited again!

Mrs. Morey finds she can entertain a great many friends at a party of this kind because they stop by for only a little while, and then are on their way. She doesn't worry about not having enough chairs; guests usually prefer to mill around. You may want to try a party like hers.

INVITATIONS

By careful searching, Mrs. Morey found just the right Christmas card to use for the invitations. It depicted a party, with people of all ages grouped around a piano singing Christmas carols. A log blazed in a fireplace, Christmas wreaths decorated doorways, lighted candles glowed from windows. Inside the card, Mrs. Morey wrote a little personal note of invitation.

> Dear Winnie and Bob
> Please come for holiday cheer on Sunday, December 19th, any time between three and seven.
> Do bring Ronnie and Gerry with you.
>
> Affectionately
> Marguerite Morey

A separate invitation went to Bob's mother, who makes her home with them.

Here is an alternate idea for invitations: most department stores sell Christmas cards with miniatures to match; send the large card to the adults, and enclose a miniature for each child. The children will be delighted to receive written invitations, while the parents will be relieved to know you really want the whole family.

If you prefer, invitations may be written on informal cards or on note paper, or they may be telephoned.

CHRISTMAS ON THE OUTSIDE

SIX-FOOT WREATH. We arrived at Mrs. Morey's party on Sunday afternoon at 5 P.M. The house was beautifully decorated outside. A tremendous wreath—6 feet in diameter—framed the large picture window. It had been made by rolling a 12-foot length of chicken wire into a wreath shape and joining the ends with wire. Outdoor Christmas lights in blue and green laced the wreath, and short evergreen twigs and holly had been inserted to hide the frame completely.

SLEIGH BELLS. A vigorous tug at the sleigh bells by the front door announced our arrival. In a moment we were welcomed, relieved of our coats, and brought into the gaiety of the party itself.

WINDOW CANDLES. The house was ablaze with candlelight. An electric candle board holding 5 white candles had been placed at each window. A 15-inch candle was used in the middle of each board, with two 12-inch ones, then two 10-inch ones, on each side. They looked quite charming with tieback curtains.

CHRISTMAS ON THE INSIDE

A lovely Christmas-party atmosphere prevailed that day.

THE SCENT OF PINE. The scent of pine from the tree and wreaths and of spices from the wassail bowl perfumed the air.

LIGHTS OUT. The Christmas trees, candles, and fire provided the only illumination.

CAROLS. Records of carols sung by a great choir, accompanied by chimes, were heard in the background.

A BEAUTIFUL FIRE. A blazing fire crackled on the hearth. Pine cones and small logs treated with chemicals to produce different colored flames had been used.

CANDLE ARRANGEMENT ON THE PIANO. A particularly effective candle arrangement graced the old-fashioned upright piano (it would be just as pretty on a grand piano or any large flat surface). A candle board was made of a 24- by 12- by 1-inch piece of lumber. Three rows of holes were drilled, each row to hold seven candles. The candle board was painted green. Mrs. Morey used 18-inch candles for the back row, 15-inch candles for the center row, and 12-inch candles for the front row.

CHRISTMAS CARDS. The wall back of the piano was covered with Christmas cards. Here's how this can be done without defacing the wall: Use long pieces of cellophane tape running vertically from ceiling to floor; fasten with tacks to the ceiling molding and to the baseboard, with the sticky side toward you. To display the cards, merely press the back of each card to the tape. If you slant the top of cards that open book-fashion a little to the right, the front pages will stay in place.

EVERGREEN BALLS. Suspended from the light fixtures by ribbon or fine wire were evergreen balls. These are fun to make: Force the sharpened ends of 6-inch evergreen twigs into a potato. (Use enough to disguise the potato completely.) Then decorate the twigs with tiny ornaments if you wish. Tie on mistletoe, and watch how popular *that* spot will be!

TREE OF CHRISTMAS BALLS. A rather modernistic tree was achieved atop a corner bookcase. An 18-inch skewer was secured in Styrofoam. Then Christmas balls in every imaginable color were strung on it by just slipping the loop of each ball over the skewer. (Place large balls at the bottom, and keep decreasing the size, ending with a few tiny balls at the top.)

GROWNUPS' REFRESHMENT TABLE

THE TABLE. In one corner of the living room, Mrs. Morey set up a buffet table for the grownups. For this she laid a round folding tabletop over a card table, then covered it with an attractive midnight-blue cloth, which she had made herself for just $2.80. (You could also use a bright-red or forest-green cloth. For directions. see "How-to" section.)

THE CENTERPIECE. The table centerpiece was most unusual. The fabric had been removed from an old umbrella, and the frame painted white. The frame was opened part way and secured with gummed tape; the handle was forced into sand in a large white flowerpot. Large bright-colored Christmas balls were wired near the end of each spoke; smaller balls were wired halfway up the umbrella to make another circle of ornaments where the sections join. A tall pointed ornament decorated the top of the "tree." Several 4- or 5-inch evergreen twigs were forced into the sand to disguise the base.

To make it even more glamorous, attach silver, pink, or turquoise tinsel to the center spoke and to the ribs of the umbrella.

THE CANDLES. At the back of the table, six white candles in holders formed a semicircle, following the curve of the table. The candleholders were novel, inexpensive, and lots of fun to make: From a sporting-goods or hardware store, buy six cork floats, each 6 inches across with a candle-size hole in the center. Paint the corks with white poster paint. Assemble a quantity of fake pearls, beads, and sequins. Using straight pins, attach these at random to the tops and sides of the cork floats.

THE REFRESHMENTS. The wassail-bowl punch was kept hot in a chafing dish and served in stout white paper mugs with handles. (You could use a large casserole over a large electric trivet.)

The Christmas-wreath punch was served in a large punch bowl with cups to match, all on a tray. Greens and small painted pine cones surrounded them.

A fascinating variety of Christmas cookies accompanied the drinks. An inviting bowl of green and purple grapes was placed in a convenient spot for nibbling.

CHILDREN'S REFRESHMENT TABLE

The long buffet in the dining room was covered with a long red runner. On it was arranged a colorful Santa Claus scene, complete with reindeer, sleigh, and a trailer filled with miniature toys.

A china Santa Claus punch bowl (you could use a colorful pitcher) was filled with hot chocolate, and little Santa mugs were grouped near it on a tray. Cookies were on Christmas-tree plates.

A friend of Mrs. Morey's had volunteered to oversee the children's refreshments and keep the cookie plates filled. This kept accidents to a minimum.

TAKE-HOME PRESENTS. A take-home present for each child spells success at almost any party. With this in mind, the hostess had wrapped a little 10-cent gift for each child and had stacked the presents around the base of the children's tree. These included whistles, paintbooks, story books, puzzles, marbles, balloons, crayons, and modeling clay.

CHILDREN'S TREE

Laughter, chatter, and squeals of delight prompted us to peek into the dining room to see what was causing the excitement.

With Mrs. Morey's niece as supervisor, each child was hard at work making an ornament to hang on the children's tree and was loving every minute!

PRELIMINARY PREPARATIONS

The dining table was covered with a plastic cloth, then with newspapers.

Plastic aprons had been made for all from a very simple pattern. (Several were cut at one time with pinking shears. See "How-to" section.)

A small Christmas tree had been set in one corner, ready to be decorated.

In the center of the table, within easy reach, were Christmas balls in all colors and sizes, Styrofoam, pine cones, red and white pipe cleaners, colored toothpicks, and construction paper in bright colors. In addition, there were gold- and silver-foil doilies, glitter, sequins, florist's wire, popcorn, blunt scissors, a stapler, gumdrops, cranberries, pins, needles, thread, etc.

TREE ORNAMENTS FOR CHILDREN TO MAKE

Some of the children needed ideas and direction; others created beautiful ornaments without help. Here's how some of the ornaments were made:

Sugar plums. Stick a small gumdrop into the end of a colored toothpick; stick the other end into a Styrofoam ball. Add about twenty more gumdrops.

Candy canes. Bend white pipe cleaners into the shape of candy canes. Twist red ones around the white ones to resemble stripes.

Cone trees. Stick cranberries, tiny Christmas-tree balls (they come on strings), and popcorn into the crevices of each pine cone. They will look like tiny Christmas trees.

Gold-foil pretties. Use two gold-foil (or silver) doilies. Place white sides together; staple. Then staple large coin sequins in different colors at random around the edges. Make a 1-inch fold across the center of the doily, then a 1-inch fold in the opposite direction; staple. This gives a ruffly, nosegay effect. (These ornaments are pretty on a tree, for they reflect the Christmas lights.)

Christmas balls and Styrofoam ornaments. Decorate them by gluing on pearls and sequins.

Bright-colored paper chains. Make from construction paper.

Popcorn chains. String popcorn with needle and thread.

As we watched the children, strains of a well-loved Christmas carol drifted in from the other room. One by one, we returned to the living room, gathered around the old piano, and joined in the singing of carols. Very soon the children joined us too. How truly the spirit of Christmas was being kept in that home!

CHRISTMAS PUNCHES AND COOKIES

CHRISTMAS-WREATH PUNCH

13 drained red maraschino cherries
13 drained green maraschino cherries
About ½ cup boiling water
Cold boiled water
  2 cans frozen limeade concentrate
  2 cans frozen lemonade concentrate
  2 No. 2 cans unsweetened grapefruit juice
    (1 pt. 2 oz.)
  2 No. 2 cans pineapple juice (1 pt. 2 oz.)
  3 1-qt. bottles ginger ale
  1 qt. water
  3 qt. chopped ice

To make wreath. Wash excess color from cherries. Arrange, alternating colors, in bottom of 1¼-quart ring mold. Pour on just enough boiling water to cover cherries; freeze solid. Then fill mold to top with cold boiled water; freeze solid. (Wreath may be made day before party.)

To make punch. In punch bowl, blend undiluted limeade and lemonade, grapefruit and pineapple juices. Just before serving, stir in ginger ale, 1 quart water, ice. Then unmold wreath on top of punch, first setting mold briefly in a little hot water. Makes about fifty punch-cup servings.

WASSAIL BOWL

1 gal. apple cider
1 cup light- or dark-brown sugar, packed
1 can frozen lemonade concentrate
1 can frozen orange-juice concentrate
1 tbsp. whole cloves
1 tbsp. whole allspice
1 tsp. ground nutmeg
24 cinnamon sticks

In large kettle, combine cider, brown sugar, and undiluted lemonade and orange juice. Tie cloves and allspice in cheesecloth; add to cider, along with nutmeg. Simmer, covered, 20 minutes. Remove and discard bag.

Serve hot, in punch cups, with cinnamon stick in each cup. Makes twenty-four punch-cup servings.

YULE LOGS

1 cup margarine
½ cup confectioner's sugar
2½ cups flour
½ tsp. cinnamon
1½ tsp. vanilla extract
1½ cups finely chopped walnuts

Blend soft margarine with the dry ingredients which have been sifted together. Add vanilla and walnuts. Roll small amounts of dough between your fingers, so that they resemble small logs about 2 inches long. Set in icebox until chilled. Bake in 350-degree oven 12 to 15 minutes until crisp and slightly browned. Cool thoroughly, then roll in confectioner's sugar.

STARLIGHT MINT SURPRISE COOKIES

A Pillsbury recipe. Makes 4½ dozen cookies.

Sift together   3 cups sifted Pillsbury's Best Enriched Flour,*
1 tsp. soda,
½ tsp. salt.

Cream   1 cup butter (half shortening may be used); add gradually: 1 cup sugar,
½ cup firmly packed brown sugar, creaming well.

* *If you use Pillsbury's Best Enriched Self-rising Flour, omit soda and salt.*

Blend in   2 eggs unbeaten
2 tbsp. water,
1 tsp. vanilla; beat well.

Add   dry ingredients; mix thoroughly. Cover and refrigerate at least 2 hours.

Open   1 package (9 oz.) solid chocolate mint candy wafers. Enclose each wafer in about 1 _bsp. of chilled dough.

Place   on greased baking sheet about 2 inches apart.

Top   each with a walnut half.

Bake   in moderate oven (375 degrees) 10 to 12 minutes.

GUM DROP COOKIES

Beat	4 eggs.
Add	1 tbsp. cold water.
Beat in	2 cups brown sugar.
Sift together and add	1½ cups flour,
	¼ tsp. salt,
	1 tsp. cinnamon.
Mix and add	1 cup shredded gum drops,
	½ cup flour,
	½ cup chopped pecans.

Spread on greased and floured cookie sheet.
Bake ½ hour in slow oven, 275 degrees.
While still warm, spread with orange icing.
Cut in 1½-inch squares and remove from pan.

Orange icing

Melt 3 tbsp. butter
Add 2 tbsp. orange juice and 1 tbsp. orange rind.
Add just enough powdered sugar to make a thin icing.

PRELIMINARY PREPARATIONS

Several days ahead

Decorate the house inside and out. Don't forget the small children's tree.
Shop for groceries, cigarettes, candles, cocktail napkins.
Make tablecloth.
Make cookies.
Assemble material for Santa's Workshop.
Make aprons for children.
Shop for take-home presents for children and wrap attractively.

The day before

Prepare spare room for wraps.
Select carols and place near record player.
Fireplace ready to go.
House spic-and-span.

The night before

Set buffet in dining room (for children).
Prepare dining table for Santa's Workshop.

Party day

Morning:
Make wassail bowl.
Set buffet table in living room.

Just before the party:
Turn on Christmas lights, outdoors and in.
Light candles.
Start carols.
Make hot chocolate. Keep hot in top of double boiler.
Place a marshmallow in each Santa mug.
Start fire in fireplace.

"HOW-TO" SECTION

Fold

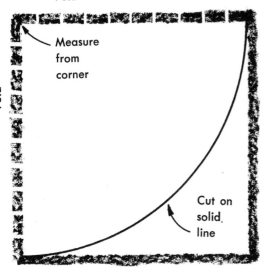

Measure from corner

Cut on solid line

Fold

HOW TO MAKE ROUND TABLECLOTH

Buy 4 yards cotton yard goods.

Cut in half crosswise.

Seam the two pieces together. Now you have a cloth 72 inches square.

Fold in half along the seam, and then in half again to make four thicknesses approximately 18 inches square. With a yardstick, measure from corner fold to the shortest side. Mark with a pencil. Keeping one end of the yardstick at the corner fold, swing it from one side of the material to the other marking with a pencil as you go so that you will have the same distance from the corner. Cut through the four thicknesses along pencil markings. When you unfold the cloth it will be circular, measuring approximately 72 inches across. Hem the edge. (When you iron it, fold in half along the seam.)

HOW TO MAKE CHILDREN'S COVER-UP APRONS

For 8

Buy 4 yards 36-inch plastic material.

Cut in half crosswise.

Fold in half, then in half again.

Draw pattern on it, then cut with pinking shears.

Staple tape on top for neckband.

Staple tape on sides for ties.

See illustration:

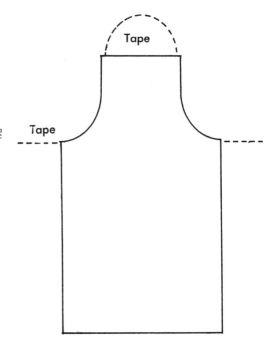

Tape

Tape

bridal Announcement tea

There is something delightfully feminine about a tea, and for that reason it seems the perfect way to tell your friends the exciting news.

You can entertain many guests at one time, as you needn't worry about seating arrangements; your friends will want to circulate from one group to another, and will stand around the beautifully set dining table to have tea and sandwiches.

SURPRISE

The party will have much more excitement and fun if the announcement comes as a surprise. If you have given the news to the local paper, ask the Society Editor to withhold the public announcement until after your tea.

A SHINING AND GRACIOUS HOME

As this is a very important occasion, you will want your home to look as lovely as possible, with everything polished to within an inch of its life. The humblest home takes on an aura of graciousness and hospitality

132

when it is bright and shining, and bedecked with flowers and candles. And speaking of adornment, don't neglect yourselves. Mother and daughter should both be becomingly gowned in their prettiest afternoon frocks.

FLOWERS SAY WELCOME

A large arrangement of green leaves and flowering branches would be lovely in the entrance hall, either on the hall table or in a large vase on the floor.

Sentimental nosegays, complete with lace and ribbons, decorate tables in the living room; a large one, delicate as a Valentine, graces the tea table (see "How-to" section).

INVITATIONS

Invitations may be written in any friendly style, and should be worded as if you were speaking to the person you are inviting. The mother of the bride-to-be issues the invitations, and of course gives no indication that the tea is "special." "Informals" are perfect for this as they carry her name on the front, and on the inside she can write simply:

> Dear Fern
> Please come to tea on Saturday, May 2nd, at 4 o'clock.
> We'll be looking forward to seeing you.
> Lovingly
> Irma

If you don't have "informals," note paper will do just as well. You could say:

> Tea
> Saturday afternoon, May 2
> 4 o'clock
> 2925-Oak St.   Irma Jahn

A ROMANTIC AND GAY TEA TABLE

Out comes your very best damask cloth in white or pastel. A careful pressing with a steam iron does wonders in bringing out the design of the cloth as well as removing the wrinkles. There should be only one crease the length of the cloth, so the pressing should be done just before setting the table. (I set my ironing board up at the end of the table and smooth the cloth onto the table as I go. Of course at this point it will be double, but when you finish ironing both sides, it is a simple matter to unfold the cloth and place it on the table. Be sure it hangs evenly on all sides.)

Possibly you have a lace banquet cloth; if so, it would be perfect for this occasion. Pink is a favorite color for brides, and a very lovely effect can be obtained by using a pink cloth under the lace (you can use a pink sheet; colored sheets in muslin are available for as little as $1.59). However, the underskirt is not necessary. There is nothing handsomer than a lace cloth on a mahogany table.

It is fine to use tea napkins if you have them; if not, use dainty paper ones. Few homes nowadays boast three or four dozen tea napkins, and such practical and attractive paper napkins are now available that no one need apologize for using them.

Of course you'll want to use the best china you can; if necessary, you may be able to borrow pieces to supplement your own set. I strongly recommend using the cup directly on a dessert plate; this gives you room for your sandwiches and other goodies, so that only one plate and cup need be used.

Candlelight is so romantic that we're determined to use candles, even if we have to pull the shades down. If you carry out the nosegay idea for your centerpiece, I think candles placed in a circle around the nosegay would be effective. Tall pink tapers add a stately charm, and if you don't have a number of matching low candlesticks, you might like to know that you can get glass ones for 10 cents in most variety stores. It would probably take ten or twelve candles to encircle the centerpiece. One of the attractions of the circle idea is that it suggests the wedding ring. If you prefer to have the candlestick bases concealed, cover them with greens.

Silver, glass, or china plates or platters are used to hold the sandwiches, small cakes, or cookies, and compotes are used for candies and nuts. Use doilies under the sandwiches or cookies. (See similar tea table in photo.)

ANNOUNCING THE ENGAGEMENT

As the girls enter the dining room to have tea, they see quantities of silver-edged pink hearts (see "How-to" section) scattered at random down the length of the table. This is the first indication that there is something "special" about this party. Each guest is told to take a heart, and he discovers that it opens up like a locket to reveal the names "Mary" on one side and "Joe" on the other. Pieces of confetti which have been concealed inside the hearts flutter to the floor or table, adding to the gaiety and excitement.

I imagine everything will come to a standstill for a few moments while the bride is embraced and showered with good wishes.

Photo by Syzdek; table setting by B. Altman & Co.

Bridal
Announcement
Tea

CLOTH   White organdy over pink

NAPKINS   White linen

CHINA   Tea-and-toast sets in bone china in various pastel colors

SILVER   Kirk's Repoussé teaspoons

CENTERPIECE   Nosegay design in blue bachelor buttons and white pompons in a silver bowl, half circled by tall pink candles in silver candlesticks

SERVING PIECES   Coffee service, footed sandwich plate, and compotes, all in silver plate

MISCELLANEOUS   News of the engagement is revealed in the little hearts which open up like lockets

Teatime

* Open-faced Cucumber Sandwiches

* Shrimp Salad Sandwich Rounds

* Watercress Cornucopias

* Heart Cookies, Pink Peppermint Frosting

* Rowena's Orange Nut Bread

* Swedish Cakes   * Bourbon Balls

Coffee

or

Bouquet of Spice Tea
(a blend of Ceylon Tea, Orange Peel,
Sweet Spice)

* Starred items will be found in recipe section.

RECIPES

OPEN-FACED CUCUMBER SANDWICHES

Wash cucumber and dry.

With a fork, make ridges from one end to the other through the rind.

Slice cucumber thin, leaving the green rind on.

Remove crusts from slices of a fresh sandwich loaf. Butter lightly.

Cut each slice in 4 squares.

Place a slice of cucumber on each square.

Sprinkle with Lawry's Seasoned Salt.

WATERCRESS CORNUCOPIAS

Watercress	Paprika
Mayonnaise	Very fresh sandwich loaf

Chop watercress fine; add a little mayonnaise and a sprinkle of paprika.

Cut crusts from bread. Spread bread with watercress mixture.

Starting from one corner, roll tightly like a cornucopia.

Secure with toothpick if necessary (remove picks before serving). Garnish with a tiny piece of watercress tucked into wide end.

SHRIMP SALAD SANDWICH ROUNDS

1 lb. shrimp, fresh, cleaned and cooked
1 tbsp. onion, minced
1 tbsp. celery, minced
1 tbsp. green pepper, minced
2 tsp. lemon juice
1 tsp. lemon rind grated
5 drops Tabasco sauce
¾ cup mayonnaise
Salt and fresh ground pepper to taste
2 fresh sandwich loaves

Grind shrimp in food chopper.
Mix together all ingredients.
Cut circle from each slice of sandwich loaves.
Place a teaspoon of shrimp on each round;
   top with another round.

❨ *Arrange sandwiches on serving plates as you make them. Cover plates securely with Saran Wrap so that the sandwiches will not dry out.*

HEART COOKIES
WITH PINK PEPPERMINT FROSTING

3 cups sifted flour   1 egg unbeaten
   (all-purpose)   ½ lb. margarine
½ tsp. baking powder
⅔ cup sugar

Sift flour and baking powder together; set aside.
Cream sugar and margarine together, then add egg.
Beat well. Gradually add dry ingredients and stir until well blended. Divide into quarters. Roll ¼ inch thick on lightly floured board. Cut out with heart-shaped cookie cutter. Bake on ungreased baking sheet in medium 350-degree oven, until slightly browned, 12 to 15 minutes. When cool ice with pink peppermint frosting.

Pink peppermint frosting

To 1 package confectioner's sugar, add a little hot water, just enough so that the icing will not be runny. Add a few drops red coloring. Be careful with this; try to get a delicate shell pink. Add a few drops peppermint extract. Ice the cookies.

If desired place a silver dragee in the center of each.

ROWENA'S ORANGE NUT BREAD

Juice and rind of 1   2 eggs
   large orange   2 cups flour
½ cup sugar   ½ tsp. salt
½ cup raisins   1 tsp. soda
½ cup shortening   ⅔ cup milk
1 cup sugar   ½ cup nuts

Squeeze the orange, and to the juice add ½ cup sugar.
Set aside.
Put raisins and orange rind through food chopper, medium blade.

Sift salt, soda, and flour.
Cream the shortening and sugar. Add eggs.
Add the flour alternately with the milk. Add the orange-raisin mixture. Add nuts.
Bake in loaf pan 1 hour in 350-degree oven.
   Be sure it is done. Test with a toothpick.
While still hot, pour orange syrup over cake and let stand.

Orange syrup

(½ cup sugar mixed with the juice of 1 orange.)

When ready to serve, slice and butter if desired. For a tea I usually cut each slice in three portions.

SWEDISH CAKES

1 cup butter
½ cup brown sugar
2 egg yolks
2 cups flour
1 tsp. salt
1 cup nuts chopped very fine

Cream the butter and sugar.

Add egg yolks, flour, and salt and beat well.

Form into small balls, dip into stiffly beaten egg white, then into chopped nuts.

Let cook 8 minutes in 350-degree oven, then take out and make a small indentation (with thimble) in the top of each cookie. Put back in the oven and cook until delicately browned. (The nuts should be lightly toasted.)

When cool, fill the indentation with a dab of jam or jelly.

These are truly delicious.

BOURBON BALLS À LA DUPLANTIS

Good news, no cooking involved

2 cups crushed vanilla wafers
¼ cup bourbon
2 tbsp. white Karo
1 cup chopped pecans
2 tbsp. cocoa
1 cup powdered sugar for rolling

Mix ingredients thoroughly, and roll into marble-size balls. Roll in powdered sugar until well-coated. These improve with age if kept in a tightly sealed container.

SERVICE

A tea service at one end of the table and a coffee service at the other work out well for a large tea.

It is customary to ask the most prominent women present to pour at a tea because it is considered an honor. If it is a very large tea, you might invite several guests to pour. A little chart like this will be convenient:

TEA		COFFEE
Mrs. G. Shapter	3:30–4	Mrs. R. Brookings
Mrs. R. Morris	4–4:30	Mrs. L. Bellis
Mrs. P. Ashley	4:30–5	Mrs. J. Berryman

At the time you extend the invitation, tell them you'd like them to pour and state the time so that they will be there at that hour.

A person with a gift for small talk is an asset in this capacity for she will chat for a moment with each guest as she is pouring. She either will ask them how they want their tea or coffee, and serve it to them, or will merely pour it, and invite them to help themselves to cream, sugar, or lemon slices.

If the tea is a small one, the hostess presides at her own table. In this case it is more gracious for the hostess to add the cream or sugar as desired.

It is a great help to have either a party maid or a member of the family or close friend keep the sandwich and cookie plates replenished. Each guest serves herself. Plates of sandwiches or sweets can be passed around as well. Remove used plates, cups, and napkins as they are set down in order to keep the room as neat as possible.

SHOPPING LISTS

Grocery list *

Cucumbers	Watercress
Pecans	Saran Wrap
Sandwich loaves	Margarine
Shrimp	Peppermint extract
Onions	Confectioner's sugar
Celery	Orange
Green pepper	Nuts
Lemon	Raisins
Mayonnaise	Vanilla wafers

* Does not include staples.

Miscellaneous list

Flowers and greens	Cigarettes
Candles	Material for heart
Paper napkins	announcements

So that you will not forget anything, check the Party Plan, pages 7–10 of this book. Make up a schedule for Party Day.

"HOW-TO" SECTION

NOSEGAY CENTERPIECE FOR TEA TABLE

You will need:

1 large round tray or service plate
3 "dividers" of various sizes, see below
Small flowers in two or three colors, just the heads

To make dividers, cut 3 strips from thin cardboard such as a laundry shirtbox, the

first   18 inches by ½ inch

second   22 inches by ½ inch

third   26 inches by ½ inch

To make a circle of each one, staple ends together (or sew).
Place circles one inside the other.
Place them on a round tray, or plate slightly larger than the largest circle. (You may have to alter the sizes to fit your container.)

The circles act as a guide in keeping the flowers separate in three different sections.
Use whatever combination of flowers you wish. I usually use pale blue bachelor buttons in the center, pale pink geranium buds * in the center row, and rose geranium buds in the outer row. Cover the edge of the plate or tray with green leaves. Arrange lacy paper doilies around the outside of the tray. If you wish, you can attach a bow and ribbons to the nosegay.

* Geranium blooms, half open, are beautiful. They resemble miniature roses. One great advantage is that they remain fresh even when out of water. A local nursery is the best source if you don't have them in your own home. My florist sells them to me for 5 cents each clump. There are usually several buds and blooms in one clump.

DOUBLE HEART ANNOUNCEMENTS

Place this pattern on a piece of pink art paper. Trace, then cut out. Fold on dotted line. You will notice that it resembles a locket. On the left side write your name, on the right side your fiancé's name. On the outside, glue around the heart outline, then sprinkle with silver glitter. Make one for each guest.

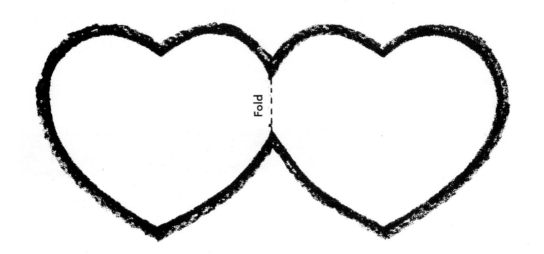

Fold

june wedding

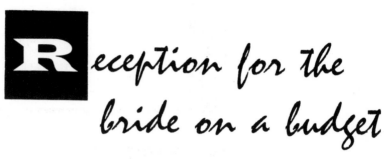

Reception for the bride on a budget

A simple pretty wedding reception at home, with family and close friends, is often a more successful party and more enjoyable to all than a lavish affair at restaurant or club.

Your guests will know you and one another well, which will eliminate feelings of tension. On this of all days you should be happy and serene. It should be an occasion of joy and spiritual beauty, and those closest to you will want to be there to share it with you.

With a little planning and a nominal amount of work, a reception can be given on a very limited budget, without sacrificing dignity and good taste. I believe you will find that despite the work involved, you will be more rested than if you planned the wedding on a more lavish scale, which always involves so many conferences. Only three things will require much time—making the wedding cake, making the rainbow petit fours, and stitching the cloth for the table.

This reception will cost about $35 for 35 guests. It will be suitable following an afternoon or evening wedding, and will be equally effective indoors, on a terrace or porch, or in the garden.

Menu

Wedding Cake   *Sparkling Punch*

Rainbow Cupcake Petit Fours

Pastel Mints   Salted Nuts

Coffee

* Recipes for starred items can be found at end of article.

BUDGETS

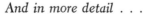

BUDGET FOR WEDDING RECEPTION FOR 35 GUESTS

Wedding cake	$ 2.75
Sparkling punch	3.00
Rainbow petit fours	.90
Pastel mints	1.00
Salted nuts	1.50
Coffee	2.00
Tablecloth and underskirt	6.35
Paper plates and napkins	1.80
Candles	1.70
Flowers and greens for cake and room decorations	7.00
Paid helper	7.00
(This will vary according to location)	
Total	$35.00

And in more detail . . .

5 cake mix at 35 cents	$ 1.75
Almonds	.50
Frosting	.50
5 ginger ale at 30 cents	1.50
5 frozen lemonade	1.00
10 eggs	.50
1 cake mix	.35
Frosting	.55
Mints 3 for $1.00	1.00
Nuts, 2 cans at 75 cents	1.50
Coffee	2.00
5 yds. nylon organdy at 90 cents	4.50
Flannelette sheet 70 by 90 inches	1.85
Plates, 4 pkgs. at 25 cents	1.00
Napkins	.80
Candles for table	1.20
Candles for living room	.50
Flowers	7.00
Paid helper	7.00
Total	$35.00

If the bride decides to use wedding cake boxes, they will cost about 15 cents each, and are usually available in pastry shops.

SAMPLE SCHEDULE

4:00 Wedding ceremony.
4:30 to 5.00 Receive the guests.
5:00 to 5:30 Cake-cutting ceremony and toasts to the bridal couple.
5:30 to 6:00 Circulate among guests. View gifts on display in spare room.
6:00 to 6:45 Bride throws bridal bouquet, then changes to street clothes.
6:45 to 7:00 Kisses and good-byes. It's time to duck the confetti and rice as bridal couple races to car.

PREWEDDING PREPARATIONS

A wedding is such a gala, exciting affair that your family and friends want to have an active part in it and are flattered that you ask them. Your reception will go more smoothly if you arrange beforehand to have:

1. One person to decorate cake with fresh flowers.

2. One or two to keep buffet table replenished (in addition to paid helper).

3. One to direct guests to room set aside for wraps.

4. Two or three persons to circulate among guests to make sure that no one is neglected.

5. One person to assume responsibility of record player. (Good job for a man.)

6. A woman to preside at the coffee service and a man to preside at the punch bowl.

PAID HELPER

One paid helper will do wonders for your peace of mind, and we've made allowances for this in setting up the budget. She should be on duty during the wedding, making last-minute preparations. Then it is her responsibility to keep the buffet table replenished. She will wash the dishes and put things away later. Note: When the bride is arranging the reception, and doing some of the work herself, it is doubly important to have as much done as possible well ahead of time, so that her mind will be at rest.

INVITATIONS

For a small, informal wedding, it is not necessary to send engraved invitations. More appropriate is a short, handwritten invitation by the bride's mother, such as:

> Dear Irene
>
> Augusta and Keith are being married on Saturday, June 15th, and we are having a small reception at home for them afterwards at 4.30. Do hope that you and George will be able to be with us.
>
> Affectionately
> Eleanor Fairbourn

Extend invitations at least two weeks in advance.

DAINTY BRIDAL TABLE

For this wedding, we pushed the dining table against the picture window overlooking the garden. The buffet table was almost as beautiful and radiant as the bride herself.

The white cloth was made of flocked nylon organdy yard goods. It had delicate white flowers with lacy green tendrils and leaves. We bought 5 yards, cut it in half crosswise, then seamed it down the center to make a cloth 72 inches wide and 90 inches long. (This material was bought at a variety store yardage department, and is also obtainable through mail order catalogues.) For a petticoat, we used a flannelette sheet. Our bride can use the cloth later for afternoon teas and luncheons.

WEDDING CAKE CENTERPIECE

The splendid three-tiered cake graced the center of the table. Each tier was encircled with tiny fresh flowers. We used pink geranium blossoms, half open, which resemble baby roses. (Other flowers that would be suitable and do not wilt out of water are: rosebuds, snapdragon buds, lilies-of-the-valley, delphinium blossoms, or stephanotis.) The top of the cake was decorated with a matching spray of flowers arranged in a small bouquet.

Good-looking paper plates, a white floral design on white, were placed in front of the cake. To the left of them were white paper napkins. To the right were forks. On either side of the cake were the petit fours in a rainbow of colors. Fresh deep purple violets were placed here and there among the cakes. Salted nuts and mints in silver compotes were placed toward the front of the table.

At one end of the table was the punch service, at the other the coffee service. (Cups were set directly on plates thus eliminating the need for saucers.)

Candles are pretty for a late afternoon or evening wedding, and we used seven tall ones in star-shaped glass holders at the back of the table.

Trailing ivy was fashioned into a garland and secured on the cloth overhang at the corners and in the center. Tendrils of ivy wreathed the cake, candlesticks, and punch bowl.

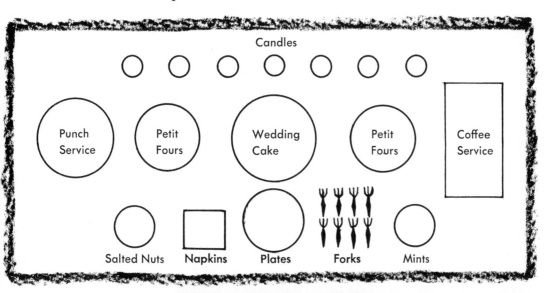

Candles

Punch Service — Petit Fours — Wedding Cake — Petit Fours — Coffee Service

Salted Nuts — Napkins — Plates — Forks — Mints

FESTIVE ATMOSPHERE

As far as possible, clear the living room of excess furniture, for this will be mainly a stand-up affair. However, a few chairs should be arranged in a cozy circle for elderly guests. A close friend should be asked to attend to their needs and see that they are not isolated.

Two or three bouquets should be sufficient: possibly a large vase in the hall filled with flowering branches and two bouquets in the living room. Choose flowers that will blend with the colors of your room, preferably all in one color or varying shades of one color, such as shades of pink to rose. Flowering branches give a light, airy, springtime feeling, and could be used as background for your other flowers. One-half dozen flowers, tastefully arranged with plenty of greens, are prettier than a profusion of flowers carelessly stuck in a vase. Flickering candles in a candelabrum will be enchanting placed in living room or hall.

Sweet music. Music adds to the gaiety of any party and especially to a wedding. A pianist, accordionist, or guitarist is ideal. Second choice is a record player softly playing sweet music throughout the reception.

RECEIVING LINE

At a small informal reception, the bride's mother as hostess receives the guests with the bride and groom. The others in the wedding party mingle informally. When all have extended best wishes to the couple, the bride's mother leads the way to the buffet.

If the ceremony as well as the reception is held in the home, the wedding party may simply turn around after the ceremony to receive best wishes. In this case, the bride's mother would move to the head of the line.

CAKE-CUTTING CEREMONY

A silver cake knife, its handle decorated with white satin ribbon, is used. The groom's right hand covers the bride's right hand as they cut together the first slice, which they share in order to symbolize the sharing of their lives.

To dream on

When everyone is served, the cake may be removed to the kitchen and a small piece placed in each wedding-cake box; the box is then tied with white or silver ribbon and placed on a tray near the door for guests to take home.

TOAST TO THE BRIDE

When all guests have been served punch, the best man proposes a toast to the bride, usually followed by other toasts. As you know, the one for whom the toast is proposed does not drink, but simply acknowledges the honor with a smile.

WEDDING GIFTS ON DISPLAY

Wedding gifts on display are a pretty sight, and if you can set them out in a spare room, by all means give your friends and family the pleasure of seeing them.

Cover a table or long chest with a tablecloth or other attractive material. A tiered effect shows the gifts off to better advantage. This can be accomplished by covering gift boxes or cartons with matching gift-wrap paper in white or silver, or with material matching that used on the table. Be careful to write a description of each gift and the donor's name in a book, then remove the cards before displaying gifts.

PHOTOGRAPHS

You will no doubt want candid pictures of the highlights of the reception. These may be taken by a friend who is a good amateur photographer. They can be either in black and white or in color.

Press notices. Mail to newspapers well in advance.

THE BRIDE THROWS HER BOUQUET

Just before the bride leaves the room to change into street clothes, she assembles her bridesmaids and other unmarried friends around her, then turns her back to them, and throws her bouquet over her shoulder. Tradition has it that the one lucky enough to catch it will be the next bride.

In the excitement and rush it is easy for the bride and groom to forget the most important people there—their parents. The couple can give great pleasure if each of them takes the time to quietly say good-bye to his or her parents alone.

THERE THEY GO

Guests have been well supplied with mysterious little packages, and amid hasty good-byes and kisses the bride and groom are showered with rice and confetti to speed them on their way.

HAPPY HONEYMOON!

RECIPES

WEDDING CAKE

You will need:

1 set tier-cake pans. (The pans I used measure 13½ inches, 10½ inches, 7½ inches. They are aluminum and cost $3.50 per set. Also available are tin ones, set of 4 for $1.50.)
5 pkgs. white cake mix.
1 6-oz. pkg. shelled almonds.

Step by step:

1. Set oven at 350 degrees.
2. Grease bottoms of pans well with vegetable shortening.
3. Out of heavy brown paper, cut liners for each. (Run a pencil around the bottom of each pan, then cut about one-quarter inch inside of line.) Place liners in pan, then grease generously.
4. Blanch the almonds. (Place in water, bring to a boil, then slip off skins.) Chop finely.
5. For bottom layer: Prepare 2½ packages of cake mix, reducing the amount of liquid by one-third. Add one-half of the almonds. Bake approximately 70 minutes.
6. For middle layer: Prepare 1½ packages cake mix, reducing liquid by one-third. Add one-half of the remaining nuts. Bake approximately 60 minutes.
7. For top layer: Prepare 1 package cake mix, reducing liquid by one-third. Add remaining nuts. In the center of the pan

place a frozen fruit juice tin from which the label has been removed. Grease well inside and out. Place a small amount of batter in the tin to act as ballast, then pour remaining batter around it. Bake about 50 minutes. (A small vase of flowers will fit into the hole in top later.)

([Allow from 2 to 3 hours for cakes to cool before removing from pans. Then very carefully remove brown liners. Place one layer on top of the other, top sides up.

ROSE-FLAVORED FROSTING
FOR WEDDING CAKE

4 egg whites
3 cups sugar
3 tsp. light corn
  syrup

¾ cup cold water
2 tsp. rose extract

Combine ingredients, except rose extract, in good-sized utensil set in pan of boiling water. Blend well, then beat with rotary or electric beater until the frosting forms peaks (7 to 10 minutes). Remove from heat, add rose extract, then beat until of spreading consistency. Pour frosting over the top of cake, guiding the frosting with a rubber spatula over the tiers until entire cake is frosted. (If you are going to put a vase in the hole in the top for flowers, frost the outside of the vase too.) The layers are stacked on top of one another before frosting. There is no frosting between layers as this would tend to make the top layers slip.

To decorate. Tiny pink and blue flowers are placed alternately around each tier, around the edge of the top layer, and a small arrangement of the same kind of flowers in the vase in center top. This should be done by one of your assistants just before the wedding.

SPARKLING PUNCH
To serve 35

5 quarts ginger ale
5 quarts lemon sherbet

Pour ginger ale into punch bowl first. Then add an equal amount of lemon sherbet. Stir. Mix until there are only small pieces of sherbet floating. (It is important to make it in this order as it might break the glass punch bowl if you put in the sherbet first.) The advantage of this recipe is that it can be made up easily as you need it, and there is no ice problem.

EASY HOMEMADE LEMON SHERBET *

To make 1 quart:

 1 5-oz. can frozen lemonade
 3 cans water
 2 eggs, whites only

Freeze to a mush, then add stiffly beaten whites of 2 eggs. Beat with a rotary or egg beater and return to freezer or ice compartment.

* The budget was based on this.

CHAMPAGNE PUNCH FOR 35

Alternate

 3 qts. ginger ale
 3 qts. lemon sherbet
 4 bottles champagne

RAINBOW CUPCAKE PETIT FOURS

Makes 6 dozen

1 package cake mix, made according to directions on package, in small muffin tins measuring 1¾ inches across.

Grease well then add about 1 tsp. in each cup. Bake approximately 15 minutes.

Icing. Mix confectioner's sugar with hot water until the mixture will pour. Should be like thick honey. You will need about 3 packages of confectioner's sugar. Make up one recipe at a time.

Suggestions on colors and flavoring:

 Pink .... rose flavoring
 Pale green .... peppermint
 Pale yellow .... lemon
 Pale blue ..... almond
 Lilac .... raspberry
 White .... vanilla

To ice, place tiny cupcakes upside down on oven rack placed over shallow pan. Dribble icing from a teaspoon held above the cakes. Move in circles so that icing flows down all sides and completely covers. Icing which flows off into pan may be scooped up and used over again. Let dry before removing to plate. If you wish, decorate tops with cake decorating tube in contrasting colors. Arrange on serving plate and tuck fresh blossoms here and there.

SHOPPING LISTS

Groceries

6 boxes white cake mix
1 6-oz. pkg. shelled almonds
1 doz. eggs
5 large bottles ginger ale
5 small cans frozen lemonade concentrate
3 boxes confectioner's sugar
2 small boxes mints
2 large cans salted nuts
2 lbs. coffee
Rose extract

Miscellaneous

Material for cloth, 5 yds
White flannelette sheet, 72 by 90 inches
Paper plates *
Paper napkins *
Candles for table and for living room
Flowers for decorating living room and hall,
  and for decorating wedding cake
* Get the best quality available.

SCHEDULE

Two or three weeks in advance

Extend invitations.
Engage paid helper.
Notify newspapers of the wedding.

Several days ahead of time

Order flowers and greens to be delivered the
  morning of the wedding.
Ask friends and members of the family to
  assist you in the various tasks. Designate
  one job for each.
Decorate the table or chests in spare room
  where gifts are to be displayed.
Decorate the cake knife.
Make arrangements with a friend to take
  candid pictures.

Best man should be reminded by someone
  about the toast to the bride. He may
  want a day or two to prepare the toast.

The day before the wedding

Make cake. Possibly a close friend or mem-
  ber of the family will help here.
Set the bridal table.
Tack up menu in kitchen.
Make list of jobs for paid helper.

Wedding day

Arrange flowers.
Decorate cake.
Light candles.

Bride's first buffet supper

"Mary, I'm really proud of your cooking, and the way you've decorated the apartment. I'd like to have our friends see how well you've done. What do you say to our having three other couples over to dinner a week from Saturday night? Let's make it special."

All this from your best beau in the most offhand manner.

Eight for dinner! Help!

Wish we could tell you that giving a party is a breeze, Mary; but the next best thing is to help you map out a campaign so that you will be fresh as a daisy on party day. By following the schedule to the letter, you will be ready and waiting in your prettiest at-home costume when the doorbell rings announcing your first guests. Only if you enjoy the party yourself will your guests enjoy it. Most pre-party nerves are caused not so much by the work involved as by the apprehension that you are forgetting something. By following the party plans described here, you will eliminate that possibility to a great extent. It is really fun once you get into the swing of it, and honestly now, haven't you been dying to show your beautiful wedding presents in action?

PARTY ATMOSPHERE

Setting a party mood is almost as important as the food you serve. The flickering light of candles, the soft strains of romantic music, the glow of a fire on the hearth, and the fragrance of flowers all add a welcoming note to your own cordiality. You want your party to go smoothly and to have just the right touch of sophistication without being pretentious.

Menu

In planning your menu, the first requisite is to have food that can be prepared in advance, and will require a minimum of last-minute preparation. Here is just such a menu:

Choice of Spiced Tomato Juice Cocktail

or

Old-fashioneds

Assorted Nibbler Crackers

* Easy East India Curry

* Fluffy Baked Rice

* Seven Condiments

* Tossed Greens with Roquefort Dressing

Heated, Buttered Rolls

Orange-Lemon-and-Lime Sherbet Parfaits

Coffee

* Starred items will be found in the recipe section.

It was in Guam, in the Mariana Islands, that I was first introduced to that delicious, exotic dish known as East India curry. At that time it was not often served here. Fortunately, this has been remedied, for more and more hostesses have discovered what a festive, satisfying, and very pretty dish it is on the buffet party table.

At first, I was mystified to hear the curry called ten-boy curry, twelve-boy curry, even fifteen-boy curry. It was explained to me in this way: in the Orient, after the curry is served over the rice, a procession of boys files in, each boy bearing a different condiment. If twelve condiments are used, twelve boys are needed to serve them. The greater the number of condiments, the more elegant the meal.

THE TABLE

If you are fortunate enough to have beautiful linens and china, you will of course want to use them for this special occasion. However, our curry menu lends itself most attractively to an informal table setting as well.

One clever hostess, for example, whose specialty is curry, achieves a slightly oriental effect by covering her buffet table with a bamboo shade. (Such a shade can be bought for about $2.00 in department stores. Or you can get a similar effect by using bamboo place mats, placed end to end, runner style, down the center of the table.) Then she pushes the table against the wall, and decorates the far end of it, leaving the rest free for serving dishes.

As a centerpiece, she uses a long brass planter filled with various kinds of leaves. (If you don't have a long planter, try a row of three or four matching pots of growing plants, set in saucers or on coasters.) Then she carefully separates the individual florets of two or three gladiolus stalks and tucks them among the green leaves. As an alternate she uses pompons. Two wooden candle-sticks are placed at each end of the centerpiece.

The silverware is rolled up in the napkins, which are of ginger-colored linen. Bells of Sarna placed between the napkins give an authentic East India look.

She chose Spode's "Indian Tree" for the china which provides good color contrast to the handsome wooden accessories. In addition to the candlesticks are a wooden, boat-shaped salad bowl, a wooden salt and pepper set, and wooden salad servers.

She uses double chafing dishes in brass which are perfect for the rice and curry. Separate bowls for the condiments are on a tray adjacent to the curry. (If you have a set of small salad bowls they are excellent for this purpose.) Gay as butterflies are the bright-colored Chinese soup spoons used for serving the condiments. In addition, there is a reed basket for rolls and a covered brass bowl for candied ginger.

See the photograph of this charming table on the next page.

SCHEDULE

FIRST PLANS

1. Discuss all the party plans with your husband. Decide together on the guest list, date and time of the party, and other details. You will find that he will be more enthusiastic and relaxed about the whole affair if he knows what and whom to expect.

Photo by Syzdek; table setting by B. Altman & Co.

**East India
Curry Table**

CLOTH   Bamboo shade

NAPKINS   Ginger linen, with silverware rolled up inside. The napkins are separated by Bells of Sarna.

CHINA   Spode's Indian Tree (russet on white)

CENTERPIECE   Long brass planter filled with a variety of leaves. Pompons are tucked in at the base.

CANDLES   Long white ones in two pairs of wooden candlesticks

SERVING DISHES   Double chafing dish in brass. Condiment bowls on a tray with Chinese soup spoons. Boat-shaped wooden salad bowl, wooden salad servers and salt-and-pepper set. Reed basket for rolls and brass bowl for candied ginger.

◖ *Do you notice that there is definitely an East Indian feeling here, even though most of the accessories are contemporary?*

2. Extend the invitations by telephone well ahead of time. This usually proves more practical than sending written invitations, for at least you know immediately how many to expect. Plan your party for 7 o'clock.

3. Lest something be forgotten, jot down each of the following:

Names of guests.

Menu and recipes to be used.

Shopping list: groceries, flowers, candles, mints, cigarettes, paper cocktail napkins, etc.

Table setup: cloth, napkins, china, centerpiece, candles, silver, etc.

Schedules for party day and days before.

Serving plan.

SEVERAL DAYS AHEAD

1. Shop for the groceries and other party supplies; order gladioli.

2. Make sure your party clothes and your husband's are in order.

3. Check the silver, china, and glassware you'll need. Polish and wash if necessary.

4. Select records for your record player; light music will add to the gaiety of the evening.

5. Make and refrigerate Roquefort dressing.

THE DAY BEFORE

1. Early in the day, cook chicken; remove meat in large pieces from bones; then refrigerate as in recipe for curry.

2. See that each and every room is spick-and-span.

3. If you have a fireplace, see that it is cleaned out and ready.

4. Check your ice supply.

5. Tack up the menu and schedule for the party day.

6. If you're using a tablecloth, be sure it's pressed with a single crease down the middle. (Pressing is easier if you place your ironing board at the end of the table and spread the cloth on the table as you iron.)

7. Cook the chicken curry; cool it quickly; turn into 3-quart ovenproof covered casserole; then refrigerate at once.

8. If you own a nest of small tables, place them in a convenient spot so your husband can whisk them out and set them wherever they're needed after the guests have served themselves. Your coffee table and end tables will help too.

9. Make the Old-fashioned mixture.

THE NIGHT BEFORE

1. Set up the buffet table as described on the preceding pages, checking off the items in this list as you do:

Cloth or bamboo shade
8 dinner napkins
8 dinner forks
Centerpiece with candles
Salts and peppers

Serving spoon for rice
Serving spoon for curry
Serving spoons for condiments
Fork and spoon for salad

2. On a side table, place water goblets and pitcher, coffeemaker, 8 demitasses or teacups and saucers, spoons, sugar bowl with lump sugar, sugar tongs, and cream pitcher.

ON THE PARTY DAY

Morning

1. Prepare 2 or more varieties of salad greens—about 2½ quarts, loosely packed; refrigerate.

2. Slash tops of 2 dozen baker's rolls, part way down, in two or three places; spread cuts with mixture of butter or margarine and garlic salt; wrap rolls in aluminum foil, ready for oven.

3. Spice the tomato juice cocktails and set in refrigerator (see Recipe Section).

4. Arrange one or two favorite kinds of cocktail crackers in large bowl or in individual bowls, one for each guest.

5. Arrange 1 pint each orange, lime, then lemon sherbet in layers in parfait or sherbet glasses; store in freezing compartment. (Or if preferred, prepare just before dessert-time.)

6. Put fresh cigarettes in containers.

7. Set out ash trays, lighters, and coasters.

8. Prepare and chop your choice of condiments (see "Recipes"); arrange in compartmented serving dish or small bowls. If hard-cooked eggs are among your choices, refrigerate them until served.

Afternoon and evening

5:00 Dress.

6:00 Tidy up bathroom; set out cleansing tissues, face powder, cotton puffs, etc. Arrange gladioli.

6:15 Light fire in fireplace if you have one.

Start heating oven to 325 degrees for curry. Set dinner plates on top of oven so they will heat.

6:20 Set out crackers and cocktail napkins on tray, leaving space for Old-fashioned glasses.

6:25 Put covered casserole of curry into oven to heat. (Heating will take about 1½ hours.) Measure coffee.

6:45 Turn on porch light if you have one. Start record player. Turn on lamps (use no strong overhead lights).

7:00 Guests start arriving. Direct them to the room you have set aside for their wraps.

7:10 When all guests have arrived, serve cocktails or tomato juice as preferred.

7:25 Put together casserole of rice; then place it in oven. Make plenty of coffee. Then join your guests.

7:45 Put rolls in oven to heat. Set out cream; fill picture with ice water; put both on side table.

8:00 Toss Roquefort dressing with salad greens. Place food and eight heated dinner plates on buffet table. (Serve curry in casserole in which it was heated after giving it a stir or two. Or serve it from chafing dish.) Light candles. Call guests to supper.

Good conversation and a little music will add the perfect touches to a delightful evening.

SERVING HINTS

One point to remember in entertaining is that you or your husband should be with the guests at all times. This takes a little teamwork, but it does make things go more smoothly. Some young friends of mine have worked out this routine for serving a buffet:

The hostess arranges food on the buffet table, then calls her guests to supper.

Guests serve themselves: First they take a dinner plate, help themselves to rice, spoon curry on top, and sprinkle on any or all of the condiments. Salad and a roll go close by on the plate. Last, each guest picks up a napkin and fork. Then each finds a place to sit, and the host sets up a small table nearby. (If anyone must hold his plate—and do try to avoid this—let it be the host and hostess, or a woman guest; men dislike lap service.)

After the main course, the hostess asks her guests to serve themselves coffee from the side table. During this interval, she removes dinner plates to the kitchen.

After the hostess returns, the host passes the tray of parfaits, each on a small plate with a teaspoon resting on the plate, at back. Later the hostess removes the used dessert dishes and coffee cups while the host passes cigarettes.

P.S. If the host is hesitant about helping with dessert, don't hesitate to ask a guest if she is a close friend. However, a word to the wise: don't allow guests to help you with the dishes; nothing breaks up the party atmosphere so quickly.

RECIPES

OLD-FASHIONEDS

The easy way

Ahead of time; make basic Old-fashioned mix this way: Slice 2 oranges, about 5 slices to an orange; then cut in half again. (If obtainable, Navel oranges are best for this, for one avoids having to cut out the seeds.)

Into a pot, pour 2 cups water, 2 cups sugar, and the sliced oranges. Boil for 5 minutes. Cool. Store in quart container. Add 1 bottle of drained cherries.

To make an Old-fashioned

Fill Old-fashioned glass with chipped ice.
Add 1 tsp. of the orange syrup.
Secure an orange slice and a cherry on a toothpick, place in glass, and add bourbon or rye to fill glass.
No dilution please. There will be enough from the melting chipped ice.
As you can see, this takes only a jiffy to make. The slice of orange is delicious, rind and all.

SPICED TOMATO JUICE COCKTAIL
Four servings

1 can (#2 size) tomato juice
2 tsp. Worcestershire sauce
1 tsp. Lawry's seasoned salt

1 tbsp. lemon juice
1 tbsp. sugar

Salt to taste.
Chill thoroughly.

EASY EAST INDIA CURRY
It has a nice mild flavor
2 qts. (8 cups) cooked chicken * or turkey
* *See instructions below.*
   in chunks
⅓ cup butter or margarine
1 cup chopped onions
1 cup chopped celery
⅔ cup flour
2 tsp. curry powder
2 tsp. salt
5½ cups milk
Speck pepper
Snipped parsley

Day before

1. Cook chicken.
For 2 quarts (8 cups) cut-up chicken: Buy 2 4½-lb. ready-to-cook stewing chickens, cut up. Place chickens in deep kettle or Dutch oven; add 3 cups hot water, 1 clove-studded onion, 3 celery tops, 1 tbsp. salt, 1 bay leaf, 1 pared carrot.

Simmer chicken, covered, about 3 to 4 hours or until fork-tender (time will vary with the bird; peek now and then, adding warm water if needed). When chickens are tender, remove; let cool slightly; then remove meat in large chunks from bones; refrigerate until needed. (Meanwhile, set kettle of broth in cold water in sink; cool quickly, changing cold water as needed; then refrigerate for later use as soup.)

2. In large kettle, melt butter; add onions and celery; cook until lightly browned. Then stir in flour, curry, salt, and pepper.

3. Slowly stir in milk, cook until thickened, stirring constantly.

4. Remove mixture from heat. Then, with fork, gently add chicken. Quickly cool mixture by setting kettle in cold water in sink and changing water as needed. When mixture is cool, turn into 3-qt. covered oven-proof casserole. Refrigerate.

Party day

About 1¾ hour before dinner, start heating oven to 325 degrees. Bake casserole of curry, covered, 1½ hour, or until heated through. Just before serving, stir *gently* with fork. Garnish top with 1-inch border of snipped parsley. Makes 10 to 12 servings.

FLUFFY BAKED RICE

3⅓ cups packaged precooked rice
3¾ cups water
1¼ tsp. salt
¼ cup butter or margarine
Paprika

1. Start heating oven to 325 degrees.
2. Into 3-quart casserole with cover, place rice, water, salt, and butter. Stir with fork to moisten rice.
3. Bake, covered, 30 minutes. Then remove from oven; uncover. Fluff up rice with fork. If desired, sprinkle 1-inch border of paprika on top of rice. Makes 8 servings.

SEVEN CONDIMENTS

Prepare your choice of the condiments below in the amounts indicated; then arrange each in separate small bowl or compartmented serving dish. (If you choose chopped, hard-cooked eggs, refrigerate them until served.)

3 chopped, hard-cooked eggs
8 chopped crisp bacon slices
1 cup crumbled canned or frozen French-fried onions
1½ cups bottled chutney
1 cup chopped peanuts
cup grated fresh or canned flaked cocoanut
½ cup chopped candied ginger

TOSSED GREENS WITH ROQUEFORT DRESSING

1½ oz. Roquefort cheese
1 tsp. salt
1 tsp. celery salt
¾ tsp. coarse black pepper
¾ tsp. dry mustard
3 tbsp. vinegar
1½ cups salad oil
¼ cup olive oil
1½ small cloves garlic, minced
2½ qt. loosely packed, mixed crisp salad greens

Several days ahead (this dressing must be made ahead to ensure full flavor):

1. In bowl, mash Roquefort cheese.
2. Stir in salt, celery salt, pepper, mustard.
3. Then slowly stir in vinegar, salad oil, olive oil. Add garlic.
4. Pour into 1-qt. bottle; refrigerate.

Just before dinner: Shake dressing well; then toss ⅔ cup of it with salad greens. (Refrigerate rest of dressing for later use.) Makes 8 servings.

GROCERY LIST *

Tomato juice	Bacon	Celery	Candied ginger
Oranges	Frozen French-fried	Curry powder	Salad greens
Maraschino cherries	onions	Parsley	Roquefort cheese
Nibbler crackers	Chutney	Precooked rice	Rolls
Chicken	Peanuts	Eggs	Sherbet
Onions	Cocoanut		

Bourbon or rye for Old-fashioned

* Does not include staples.

Happy-birthday supper for six

You have a tiny apartment, you are a working gal, but your husband's or beau's birthday is drawing near, and you want to celebrate in some small way. (The single man could give this party with equal success.)

I believe you'll find that entertaining a few at a time, say two favorite couples, will be more fun for everyone than would a large unwieldy affair.

Here is an easy-to-give supper party for six. The schedules on page 168 will be particularly helpful as you necessarily have to do all the preparation before or after working hours.

GENERAL PLAN

Type of party? Birthday supper.

Invitations? Telephoned.

Time? Seven o'clock.

Menu? Italian food.

Table decorations? Italian restaurant type.

Entertainment? Round-the-table games (see Game Section).

Dress? Informal. Girls may want to wear peasant skirts and blouses; men will be comfortably dressed in sport shirts and slacks.

Menu

* Antipasto

Choice of Vin Rosé, Tomato Juice,

or * Clam Juice Cocktail

* Italian Delight * Bread Sticks

Lettuce Chunks * Sour Cream Dressing

Eat-the-Centerpiece

(Frosted Grapes, Cheese and Crackers
in individual packets)*

Coffee

Ten o'clock Snack

Birthday Cake, Demitasse

* Starred items will be found in recipe section.

Planning a party menu which can be prepared almost entirely in advance is a *must* for anyone who works.

The recipe for this main dish, Italian Delight, is the most valuable recipe I possess. It was given to me by Frances and Roy Howell, of Los Angeles. I, in turn, have given it to friends all over the world who assure me that it is universally liked.

To obtain the rich, full flavor, make it the night before and store in the refrigerator. If there is any left over after the party, which I doubt, freeze it. It is just as delicious the second time around. The other items on the menu have an Italian flair. All are easy to prepare (see Recipe Section).

THE TABLE

You will, of course, use a dining or dinette table if you have one. However, as many apartments are furnished with only a small folding table, I'd like to bring to your attention the sturdy, round Extenda-top tables which are designed to fit over a card table.

By using one of these, you can seat six people at once with no crowding. There is room in the center of the table for candles and serving dishes, and because the table is round, chairs will not be crowded together. The top folds in the center for easy storage.

Most of us have a set of pottery, and this will be perfect for your Italian supper.

For pennies you will be able to make or buy a checkered cloth to harmonize with your dishes. I have yellow pottery, so I use a brown and white checkered cloth with brown napkins. Another attractive combination is a black and white checkered cloth, red napkins, and white pottery. The possibilities of color combinations are almost endless.

DRIP CANDLES IN BROWN BOTTLES

I use drip candles in bleach bottles (Clorox, the half-gallon size with the handle). To get the attractive multicolored drip effect:

1. Wash and remove labels from bottles; then place them on table with several thicknesses of newspapers under them.

2. Pour a little water into a frying pan. Turn heat on low.

3. Put one cube of paraffin (the kind used for canning) into each of four empty cans. Set cans in water.

4. Drop a one-inch stick of wax crayon into each can. I use green, purple, red, blue.

5. When paraffin and wax crayon are melted, stir well, then very slowly dribble it over the neck of the bottle, so that the wax runs down the sides. It will congeal almost instantly. Use first one color and then another to achieve a rainbow effect. On the night of the party use a tall drip candle in each. Light them before guests arrive.

EAT-THE-CENTERPIECE

The centerpiece serves two purposes; it is both a decoration and the dessert course. The drip candles are placed in the center of the tray; then frosted grapes are heaped up on a small platter or wicker container, together with small packets of saltines wrapped in Saran Wrap, and tiny individual pots of assorted cheeses. (Recipe for Frosted Grapes in Recipe Section.)

SUGGESTIONS ON SERVING

To keep your small room as uncluttered as possible, delay setting the table until you have finished your appetizer course.

Everything needed to set the table has been placed together beforehand. When the appetizer course has been removed, your husband lifts the table out to the center of the room, one guest puts on the cloth, napkins, candles, and centerpiece; another the silver, glasses, plates, and salts and peppers. Sugar, cream, and coffee over a candle-warmer are on a side table.

When all is ready, you whisk the food to the table, and *voilà*, you are ready.

ANTIPASTO. Arrange attractively on a round or rectangular platter or on a lazy susan. Place on a coffee table within easy reach of all. Place the wine or juice cocktails and glasses on a tray nearby. A stack of small plates and salad forks is placed by the antipasto, and guests serve themselves. Hostess removes used plates, and makes last minute preparations in the kitchen.

ITALIAN DELIGHT AND SALAD. Hostess sets a stack of plates in front of host, then brings in Italian Delight in a bake-and-serve casserole. She places this in front of him with a large serving spoon. She places the wooden salad bowl and salad servers to his right. Filled plates are passed to guests. Bread sticks in a glass mug are also passed around.

DESSERT AND COFFEE. When table is cleared, hostess transfers tray to the table and pours coffee. She passes around small plates and fruit knives. Guests serve themselves frosted grapes and crackers and cheese.

For the 10 o'clock snack she uses small china plates and after-dinner coffee cups (optional).

BIRTHDAY CAKE. A birthday isn't a birthday without a cake.

At the conclusion of the games, the hostess will dim the lights and bring in the blazing birthday cake while guests sing the traditional "Happy Birthday to You." Whether eight or eighty, the Birthday Child makes a wish on the flickering candles and blows them all out with one puff to make the wish come true. He cuts the first piece of cake, the hostess cuts and serves the rest. Guests serve themselves coffee.

(Note: After your supper, possibly your guests will help clear the table for games. This will give you a moment to stack the dishes, cover them with a clean towel, and get back to the living room. In the meantime your husband could place game equipment on the table. It should all be assembled beforehand.)

RECIExPES

ANTIPASTO

Antipasto, meaning appetizer, is the favorite first course on Italian menus. It simply means an assortment of tasty tidbits eaten leisurely as an accompaniment to wine or juice cocktails.

Choose four or five from among these, arrange on trays in attractive designs, and listen to the exclamations when you set them down in front of your guests. This dish is indeed a thing of beauty. Keep color appeal in mind as well as design.

1. Two-inch slices of celery stuffed with blue cheese.
2. Halves of deviled eggs topped by anchovy paste rosettes.
3. Small sardines on saltines topped by blobs of mustard sauce.
4. Dried beef slices spread with a combination of cream cheese and horseradish. Roll in cornucopia shape, secure with toothpick.
5. Canned artichoke hearts marinated in sour cream dressing.
6. Slices of small salami.
7. Liver pâté balls. Mix together 2 cans liver pâté, 1 tsp. finely chopped onion, 1 hard-cooked egg chopped fine, salt and pepper to taste. Chill, then roll in small balls. Small pieces of Melba toast make a good accompaniment.
8. Cucumbers, peeled, then cut in slices 1½ inches thick. Scoop out seeds, then fill with sour cream dressing.
9. Tiny beets, marinated in thin mayonnaise or French dressing, sliced onions, celery seeds.
10. Pickles, ripe olives, green olives, dill pickles; they should all be sliced thin.

Allow about four antipastos per person.

CLAM JUICE COCKTAIL

Clam juice comes in 8-oz. bottles. I personally think that it is delicious without any condiments added, but you may prefer to season it with lemon juice, celery salt, Worcestershire sauce, onion juice. Serve ice-cold with antipasto.

ITALIAN DELIGHT

Serves 8 to 10

8-oz. package shell macaroni
For the sauce you will need:
¼ lb. margarine
3 medium onions
1 bell pepper
3 cloves garlic
2 pounds ground beef
2 cans tomato sauce
1 can whole-kernel corn
1 small can mushrooms
1 cup grated cheese
1 tbsp. brown sugar
1 tbsp. Worcestershire sauce
1 tbsp. chili powder
½ cup sherry (optional)
Salt and pepper to taste

1. Cook one 8-oz. package of shell macaroni in boiling salted water. When tender, drain and let cold water run over it for a few minutes.

2. Brown the onions, bell pepper, garlic, and ground beef in the margarine. (To ensure the meat being brown and crusty, cook small amounts at a time.) Add the remaining ingredients, and mix well.

3. Combine the sauce with the cooked macaroni being careful not to break up the shells. Store in refrigerator. Heat in oven in a bake-and-serve casserole for 1 hour at 300 degrees. Should be bubbling hot. Heat with cover on casserole. This mixture should be moist, but not runny. If it seems a little dry, add a can or two of tomato sauce. To ensure full flavor, make the day before. May be frozen.

ITALIAN BREAD STICKS

The easy way

Prepare a package of roll mix according to directions. When it has doubled in bulk, turn out on floured board, and knead for a few minutes. Pinch off a piece of dough about the size of a small egg, grease your hands a little, and roll between your hands until each piece is about 10 to 12 inches long, and about ⅜ of an inch thick. Sprinkle with salt crystals or table salt. Let rise. Bake 12 to 15 minutes in 350-degree oven. Bread sticks should be light brown.

SOUR CREAM DRESSING

½ pint commercial sour cream
½ cup salad oil
1 clove garlic, put through press
¼ tsp. salt
Fresh ground pepper

(Make a day or two beforehand to insure full flavor.) Tear lettuce apart in bite sizes. Add just enough dressing to lightly coat leaves.

FROSTED GRAPES

1. Buy green seedless variety, wash, and drain well.
2. With scissors, cut into small bunches.
3. Dip in unbeaten egg white, then shake in a bag with granulated sugar. Be sure each grape is coated.
4. Store in refrigerator. Arrange on tray an hour before party time. Delicious!

AFTER-SUPPER FUN: GAMES

You'll hear the following game referred to as Dealer's Choice, Hash, Potpourri, Confetti, or Garbage. It is simply any collection of games played around a table—some of them card games, some paper-and-pencil games, some dice games. The great appeal is the variety, and the fact that you play one game for a few minutes only, then are off to the next one. All will be familiar to you, and I'm sure that some will bring back nostalgic memories of childhood. Almost all of us find it fun to occasionally turn back the years and play games we played long ago.

Add your own pet games to this list. I think you'll be surprised at the fun that even the most sophisticated will get out of it, and the hilarious rivalry to win. Either play for points, awarding one prize to the winner, or have a ten-cent prize for the winner of each game.

COOTIE

Each player is given a pencil, piece of paper, a dice, and a cup or glass in which to throw it. The object of the game is to draw a cootie complete with body, head, tail, legs, feelers, eyes.

The body is 1

The head is 2

The tail is 3

The legs are 4

The feelers are 5

The eyes are 6

You must roll a 1 for the body first before you can add the legs or tail.

You must roll a 2 before you can add the eyes or feelers.

For each 4 you may draw one leg, for each 5 you may draw one feeler.

The leader says "go" and everyone starts tossing dice at the same time. The faster you play, the more opportunity you have to win. The first one to complete the drawing wins. (If you are playing for total points, count one for each part of the body you have drawn. There are 13 in all.)

FAN TAN

The object: To get rid of all cards in your hand as soon as possible.

Deal out all the cards. The player to the left of the dealer leads with any card he chooses. For instance, he might pick the Jack of Hearts. Someone will cover it with the Queen of Hearts, then the King will be played, then the ace and so on up through the ten of hearts to finish the suit. The player of the last card then starts another suit in a different color, and so the game goes until someone runs out of cards, and calls out "Fan tan." (Note: if a player cannot change the color, he has to pass, and the next person to his left plays.)

BROKEN QUOTATIONS OR PROVERBS

This one requires a little work beforehand, but once the deck is made up, you can use it over and over. The hostess, in advance, pastes a blank piece of paper on each card of an old deck. Then she writes or prints in large letters one-third of a familiar quotation, proverb, or old saying on each card.

Examples:

A	*AND*	*ARE*
FOOL	*HIS*	*SOON*
	MONEY	*PARTED*

The play. Cards are shuffled well, then dealt around. Each player in turn takes a card from the player on his right. The winner is the one who first gets all three sections of the quotation.

Quotations that could be used:

Laugh and the world laughs with you.

Birds of a feather flock together.

Out of the frying pan, into the fire.

You cannot have your cake and eat it.

CATEGORIES

Have each guest print "HAPPY BIRTH-DAY" in a vertical column on the left side of page. Across the top name any four categories such as Animals, Food, Countries, Flowers. Guests must write examples of every category; the first letter of each example must correspond with the letter in the left-hand column. See example:

	ANIMALS	*FOOD*	*COUNTRIES*	*FLOWERS*
H	*Horse*	*Ham*	*Holland*	*Hyacinth*
A				
P				
P				
Y				
B				
I				
R				
T				
H				
D				
A				
Y				

SHIP, CAPTAIN, AND CREW

1. Five dice are used
2. Each player is entitled to three throws, but may stand on one or two throws if he wishes.
3. The player with the highest number of crew members wins the game.

To play

The 6-spot represents the ship.
The 5-spot represents the captain.
The 4-spot represents the crew.

The remaining two dice represent the number of crew members.

Now, if you were taking a cruise, you would need, first a ship, then a captain, then a crew in that order. So it is with this game. You must first throw a 6, then a 5, then a 4 before you are entitled to add the members in your crew. When you get your ship you set the 6 aside. When you get your captain, you set the 5 aside. When you get your crew, you set the 4 aside. Add the numbers on the remaining dice, and that gives you the number in your crew.

Example: The perfect throw would be if you got a 6, a 5, a 4, and two 6's.

You'd have your ship (6), your captain (5), and your crew (4).

The total of the remaining dice is twelve, which is the maximum number. In this case you would stand on one throw.

DRAW POKER

And back to cards again—this time for a game of Draw Poker with deuces and one-eyed Jacks wild.

PIG

Place in the center of the table five spoons (if you have six players). Deal the cards as far as they will go.

The object of the game is to get four of a kind—four Kings, four sevens, etc. Each player in turn takes a card from the player on his right. The play progresses around the table until someone gets four of a kind. He calls out "Pig," at which time he and all the rest of the players grab for a spoon. One will be too late to get a spoon, and he has to pay a penalty. For five minutes he has to run errands for anyone at the table, get a cigarette, bring a match, get a drink, etc.

HAWG

This is played the same way as Pig except that the first one to get four of a kind lays his finger at the side of his nose, and says nothing. As soon as the other players observe this, they do the same. The fun of this game comes in where one player will talk on and on sometimes, and keep on playing long after everyone else has caught on. He then takes over as waiter, and runs errands for five minutes. First one out wins.

ARTISTS

Equip everyone with pencil and paper. Let's see what your guests' artistic abilities are.

Each player folds his paper into three equal parts crosswise. In the top section he draws the head of either a human being, a fish, an animal, or a bird. He extends the neck down a little way into the second section. Then he folds his drawing over, and passes it to his left-hand neighbor who draws the body. He, in turn extends the body a little way into the third section, then folds it. The third artist draws the legs in the lowest space, then passes it on.

All now open up the drawings, and exhibit the results. No prize necessary.

BINGO

Let's end the games with a good quick session of Bingo. (A very reasonable set from the ten-cent store will be adequate.)

SCHEDULE

Several days ahead

Extend invitations.
Shop—see shopping lists.
Make salad dressing.
Make bread sticks and freeze.
Frost the grapes and refrigerate.
Check your linen. Press if necessary.

Polish silver, china, glassware.
Make drip-candle arrangement in bleach or vinegar bottle, the half-gallon size, or in wine bottle.
Assemble equipment for games and wrap prizes.

The night before

Prepare Antipasto.
Make Italian Delight
Assemble table setting equipment, and place in convenient location.
Check-off list for table:

    Cloth
    Napkins
    Centerpiece

Drip candles
Plates
Silver
Water goblets
Wine glasses
Salt and pepper shakers
Serving forks and spoons
Serving dishes
Cigarette urns, trays, matches
Cups and saucers on a tray

Party day, A.M.

Prepare salad ingredients and store in refrigerator.

Check ice supply.
Set out fresh cigarettes in containers.

Party day, P.M.

5:00 Home from work.
Dress.
Check bathroom. Set out Kleenex, fresh soap, extra bathroom tissue, face powder, individual lipsticks.

6:00 Remove bread sticks from freezer.
Arrange Antipasto on tray and set on coffee table
Arrange centerpiece of frosted grapes, crackers, cheese.

6:30 Heat the Italian Delight. Keep wine or juice cocktails chilled in refrigerator.

7:00 Guests arrive. Serve Antipasto and wine or juice cocktails.

7:15 Make coffee.
Toss salad. Add dressing.
Husband brings in Extenda-top table, sets it on card table, guests help to set table.

7:30 Light candles.
Set food on table and call your guests to supper.

8:30 to 10:00 Play games.

10:00 o'clock snack, birthday cake, and coffee.

SHOPPING LISTS

Grocery list *

Ingredients for Antipasto, depending on which ones you choose (see Recipe Section).

Wine or Clam Juice

Ingredients for Italian Delight:
1 pkg. (8-oz.) shell macaroni
3 med. onions
1 ball pepper
2 lb. ground beef
2 cans tomato sauce
1 can whole kernel corn
1 small can mushrooms
¼ lb. cheddar cheese

chili powder
sherry (optional)

For salad:
½ pint commercial sour cream
1 or 2 heads lettuce, depending on size

For bread sticks:
1 pkg. roll mix
Salt crystals (optional)

For dessert:
Assorted crackers
Assorted cheeses in individual jars or packets
2 lb. seedless green grapes
Birthday cake from bakery

Staples not included in this list.

Miscellaneous shopping list

Material for cloth
Wax crayons and paraffin
2 candles, drip type if available
Birthday candles
Cigarettes
Cocktail napkins
Ten-cent-store prizes

Equipment needed for games:
Deck of cards

Spoons
Deck of cards made up with broken quotations
6 dice and dice boxes (tumblers will do)
Pencils
Paper
Bingo set
Poker chips

Teens' Graduation party

Marguerite and Caroline were bemoaning the fact that after graduation their friends would be scattering to the far corners of the country, to colleges, the armed services, or to jobs. It would be fun to get them all together one more time. So the girls decided to pool their resources and give a dinner party at Marguerite's before the formal Graduation Ball.

Because the girls gave the party together (with the help of course of "Mama") it wasn't too much trouble for anyone.

HOW THEY PLANNED THE PARTY

Three weeks ahead of time, Marguerite and her mother, Mrs. Fay, and Caroline and her mother, Mrs. Beach, met over coffee and discussed the menu, table settings, service and schedules. They also discussed how they were going to divide expenses and work. Expenses were to be divided evenly, each person to keep track of what she had spent. It was also agreed that the girls would be free of any responsibility on party night. For one thing they would be in their formal gowns. In addition, they would have to be free to perform their duties as hostesses. So Mrs. Fay and Mrs. Beach agreed to prepare and serve dinner.

In view of this, the girls offered to do a greater portion of the preliminary work. Together they shopped for groceries and miscellaneous items, extended the invitations, helped put the house in apple-pie order, set the tables, and arranged the flowers.

Menu

* *Cranberry Fizz Punch*

Cheese Crackers   Salted Nuts

Tossed Green Salad   Choice of Dressings

* *Broiled Chopped Sirloin Steaks,*
wrapped in Bacon

Stuffed Baked Potatoes

Buttered Asparagus

Hot Rolls

* *Baked Alaska Pie, Flambé*

Coffee

* Starred items will be found in the recipe section.

BUFFET AND "CABARET" TABLES

A buffet table was set in the dining room. Three card tables were put up in the living room.

CLOTHS. Made of red and white checked yard goods.

NAPKINS. White, rolled up and tied with red ribbon to resemble diplomas.

CHINA. White pottery.

GLASSWARE. Dime-store red tumblers.

CENTERPIECE. Red geraniums and green leaves in ring molds. Edges were covered with small green twigs. Candles which dripped colors had been secured in green ginger ale bottles. One was placed on each table in the center of the flower ring.

From white pipe cleaners the girls had fashioned CLASS OF '57. One was propped against each centerpiece.

FAVORS. Marguerite and Caroline had made inquiries about the birth month of each guest, and had bought a horoscope (25 cents) for each one. These doubled as place cards. Names of guests were written at top. Much discussion of predicted futures got the party off to a merry start.

Check-off list for buffet table

Cloth

Centerpiece and candles

Plates

Serving dishes

Serving forks and spoons

Cups and saucers

Check-off list for "cabaret" tables

Cloth and napkins

Centerpiece and candles

Cream and sugar

Salad on salad plate

Silver

Water glasses

Salt and pepper shakers

Horoscopes, on which names are written

SERVICE

This party worked very smoothly with Mrs. Beach in charge of the food and Mrs. Fay in charge of serving and keeping the buffet replenished.

The cranberry fizz punch was served from a punch bowl into punch cups. The hostesses passed the snacks and invited the guests to help themselves.

At dinnertime, each guest served himself from the buffet and found his place at one of the small tables. Salad was on the tables, just to the left of each plate. (Crescent-shaped salad plates which fit into the curve of the plate are wonderfully convenient when you're serving the salad and meat course together.)

Hot rolls were passed after guests were seated.

When the main course was finished, plates were removed. Lights were dimmed and the baked-Alaska pie was brought in flaming. It was then cut in serving portions and served on dessert plates.

The filled coffee cup was served to each guest. Cream and sugar was on the table.

MISCELLANEOUS SUGGESTIONS

If you have a record player, arrange to have it on at least during dinner to give the desired cabaret atmosphere.

To make everything go smoothly, consult the check-off lists in the Party Plan on page 7, to make sure that you haven't forgotten anything.

Try to get some flash pictures of this party. They will become very precious to you later on. It would be a nice gesture to order a print for each guest.

An alternate idea would be to have a "Snapshot Exchange." Each person would bring a snapshot of himself for each guest.

Allow time in your schedule for the girls to primp a little before going on to the dance.

RECICPES

CRANBERRY FIZZ PUNCH

For 12

1 28-oz. bottle strawberry soda
2 16-oz. bottles cranberry juice
1 gal. apple cider
1 lime sliced thin

Chill in icebox before opening bottles.
When guests arrive, pour over block of ice in
  punch bowl.
Float thin lime slices as garnish.

BROILED CHOPPED SIRLOIN STEAKS WRAPPED IN BACON

For 12

6 lbs. chopped sirloin (preferably with fat
  removed; this way it tastes more like
  steak)
1 onion, minced (optional)
2 tbsp. melted butter
Salt and pepper
12 to 18 strips bacon

Brown the onions lightly in butter.
Mix thoroughly the meat, butter, and seasonings, working the ingredients together
  with your hands. (This will make them
  easier to shape.)
Shape into 12 steaks about 4 inches by 2
  inches. Wrap bacon around the edge, securing with toothpicks. Place steaks on a
  platter, then wrap the whole thing in
  Saran Wrap until ready to broil.

To broil steaks. Preheat oven. Place
steaks on broiler pan about 3 inches from
the flame. Broil 5 to 10 minutes on each
side depending on how well done you like
them.

BAKED ALASKA PIE FLAMBÉ

You will probably need two pies. Each one will serve 6.

For each pie you will need:

1 baked pie shell

1 qt. ice cream

Meringue for topping

4 lumps of sugar soaked in lemon extract.

Recipe for meringue

For 1 pie

3 egg whites	½ tsp. vanilla
½ tsp. salt	4 tbsp. sugar
½ tsp. cream of tartar	

Sprinkle salt and cream of tartar over egg whites.

Beat until frothy with rotary beater or electric beater.

Sprinkle sugar over surface, adding 1 tbsp. at a time and beating well between additions. Continue beating until meringue is very stiff.

To assemble Baked Alaska Pie. Fill the baked pie shell with softened ice cream, then cover with the meringue. It must be *totally* covered. Be very careful of this. Don't leave any crevices where the heat can reach the ice cream.

Bake in preheated 425-degree oven for 4 to 5 minutes until lightly browned. Place the lumps of sugar on top. Dim the lights, ignite the sugar, and bring to table flaming. It will stay lighted for only about 30 seconds so you have to work fast.

GROCERY LIST *

Strawberry soda	Chopped sirloin
Cranberry juice	Bacon
Apple cider	Baking potatoes
Lime	Frozen asparagus tips
Cheese crackers	Rolls
Salted nuts	Ice cream
Salad greens	Lump sugar
Dressing	Lemon extract

* Does not include staples.

teens'  alentine party

Recently I received a letter from the chairman of a teenage group planning a St. Valentine's Day party in a church recreation room. This is how I suggested she organize the party and still keep within her budget of $5 for all expenses except food.

ORGANIZING THE PARTY

The chairman should do as little of the actual work as posible. She will be called on to make decisions and to give her approval of the plans made by the committees. She will be more valuable to them for consultation if she's not bogged down by petty details.

Appoint one person to head each of these committees: food, decorations, entertainment, kitchen cleanup.

Ask the committee chairmen to include each member of the group on one of the committees, being careful not to overlook anyone. Don't forget, the shy girl is often the best cook. Four more reasons for including everyone are:

1. Many hands make light work;
2. The planning and preliminary preparations are often as much fun as the party;
3. Shy people have a chance to prove their talents;
4. Each person feels personally responsible for making the party a success.

Both boys and girls should be on each committee. And, to retain an element of suspense, committees should keep their plans secret—except from the chairman, of course.

One other thing: organizations seldom lend a recreation room to a young group unless an older couple comes along to accept responsibility. Sometimes two of the mothers will keep an eye on things in the kitchen, but don't expect them to do the cleanup work!

The food committee

Plans the menu.
Shops for groceries.
Prepares food.
Arranges food on the tables.
Helps serve.

The decorations committee

Plans the decorations.
Shops for materials.
Makes decorations.
Decorates the room and tables.

The entertainment committee

Plans games and novelty dances.
Assembles the equipment.
Buys and wraps prizes, if any.
Arranges for music.

The kitchen-cleanup committee

Dismantles the tables.
Discards paper plates, cups, and other paper supplies.
Washes, dries, puts away equipment.
Sweeps the floor.

TENTATIVE SCHEDULE

After school on St. Valentine's Day, the food, decorations, and entertainment committees meet at the recreation room and make their final preparations. The schedule:

6:00 Home for dinner, and dress (party-best clothes).
8:00 Party begins. Play games and dance.
9:30 Serve supper.
10:15 Dance one more dreamy dance (the kitchen-cleanup committee misses this one), then home (it's a school night).

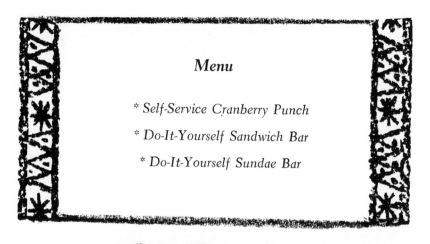

Menu

* *Self-Service Cranberry Punch*

* *Do-It-Yourself Sandwich Bar*

* *Do-It-Yourself Sundae Bar*

RECIPES

SELF-SERVICE CRANBERRY PUNCH

1 46-oz. can grapefruit juice
1 46-oz. can pineapple juice
6 16-oz. bottles cranberry juice
2 28-oz. bottles ginger ale

Combine well-chilled juices with ginger ale. Pour over ice in punch bowl. Makes about 40 punch-cup servings.

Make a sign reading SELF-SERVICE PUNCH BOWL, to greet guests as they arrive. Make enough punch so that guests may serve themselves throughout the evening.

DO-IT-YOURSELF SANDWICH BAR

The food committee sets up a separate table, buffet style, for sandwich makings. At serving time, the committee attractively arranges cold meats, cheese, peanut butter, devilled-egg mixture, tuna-salad mixture, or whatever is decided on. In addition, they set out white bread, wheat bread, butter or margarine, mayonnaise, mustard, pickles, potato chips, etc. Each person makes his own "Dagwood."

DO-IT-YOURSELF SUNDAE BAR

The food committee sets up a sundae-bar table, with chocolate syrup, marshmallow sauce, chopped nuts, cherries, etc., and large saucers and spoons. (Ice cream was purchased earlier in the evening and was stored in the freezer or ice-cube section of the refrigerator.) When it's time to serve dessert, the committee empties cartons of ice cream into large bowls, and lets each person make his own sundae.

MARDI-GRAS DECORATIONS

Try using vivid Mardi-gras colors for room and table decorations. Cerise, jade-green, bright blue, purple, and yellow can create a gay, carnival spirit that's quite in keeping with this holiday.

Hearts in blue, green, purple. From art paper, cut out hearts in all colors and sizes. Staple hearts to crepe-paper streamers, and drape them in windows and doorways. Tie colored yarn or thin wire from the chandelier to the four corners of the room. Throw ribbon (serpentine) confetti over the wires; then staple more paper hearts to the ends of the confetti.

Japanese lanterns. Borrow them; they should be hung high enough so people won't bump into them.

Spiral balloons. Choose three balloons in different colors; tie them together loosely. Tie ribbon confetti into bows and streamers; attach to the three balloons. Attach the balloon clusters to curtains or draperies or the chandelier, or anchor them to a bowl on the table or the top of the piano.

ON YOUR TABLE

Jewel tones. Use Mardi-gras colors—they are lovely with any solid-color tablecloth as a background. Paper napkins come in bright colors, with about six colors to a package; mix the colors at each table. The same goes for candles; for each table, buy one each in red, blue, orange, green, etc. Place candles equidistantly down the middle of each table, or group three together at the center.

Harlequin masks. Do provide harlequin masks, glittering and glamorous, setting one at each place as a conversation-piece favor. Also use miniature harlequin masks for place cards. To make masks: Cut out masks, 8 inches across, from bright-colored art paper. Across top of each, glue row of sequins. Brush bottom edge with glue. Sprinkle thickly with multicolored glitter. Attach hat elastic to sides. (See pages 180–181.)

"I Love You." Cutouts of "I Love You" may be pinned or stapled to the overhang of the tablecloth. To make cutouts: Write "I Love You" in large letters on a piece of light cardboard. Write over the letters again so they are about ½ inch thick. Cut out letters with pair of small sharp scissors. This is your pattern. Then trace letters onto colored art paper, and cut out. Make ten or twelve in different colors. They are effective not only on the tables, but tacked here and there as room decorations.

Heart-shaped philodendron centerpiece. The philodendron plant has heart-shaped leaves and so makes an appropriate centerpiece. If you wish, hang heart cutouts on it. From art paper, cut hearts about 3 inches across. Cut a smaller heart from each center, leaving just the outline of a heart about ½ inch wide. Brush on line of glue along heart outline; sprinkle on multi-colored glitter. Set two heart outlines of contrasting colors side by side; staple. If you wish, attach bows of narrow ribbon with long streamers that cascade down the length of the table.

PATTERN FOR CUT-OUT HEARTS IN MARDI-GRAS COLORS

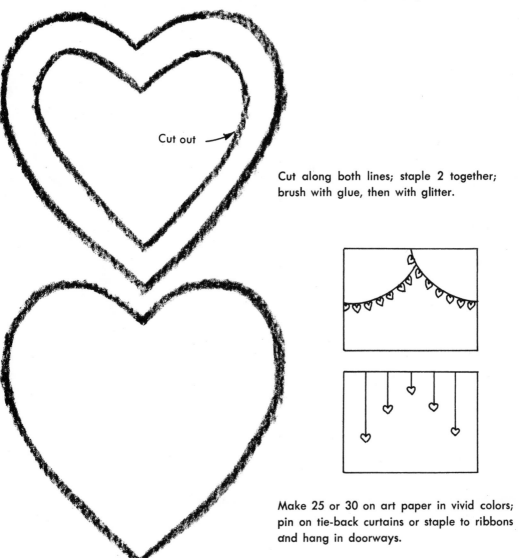

Cut out →

Cut along both lines; staple 2 together; brush with glue, then with glitter.

Make 25 or 30 on art paper in vivid colors; pin on tie-back curtains or staple to ribbons and hang in doorways.

PATTERN FOR CLOWN MASK

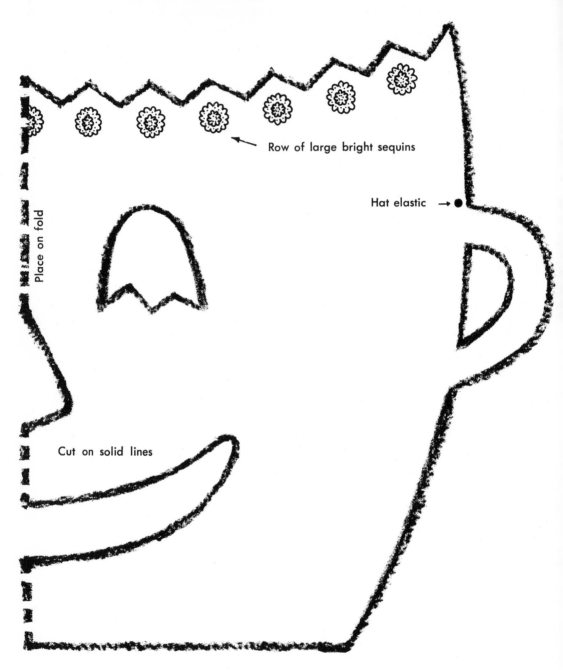

Row of large bright sequins

Hat elastic →

Place on fold

Cut on solid lines

LET'S PLAY GAMES

Although you may prefer to "just dance and play records," it's fun on special occasions such as this to play a few party games.

VALENTINE RELAY

Preliminary preparations: Place two chairs at each end of the room; place a bowl filled with red tissue-paper hearts on one set of chairs. On each of the two chairs at the other end, place an empty bowl. Supply each player with a soda straw. Players are divided into two teams.

To play the game: Members of each team line up behind their captain. At the word "go," the captains race to the opposite end of the room; each picks up a paper heart on the end of his straw by drawing in his breath, then races back to the other end of the room and deposits it in an empty bowl. Then the next player follows the same procedure. If a heart drops, the player must get down and inhale it onto the end of his straw again. First team through wins, and each member of the winning team gets a candy kiss.

DRAWING A VALENTINE

Furnish everyone with a piece of paper. Turn lights out. Ask everyone to draw a heart on the paper, put an arrow through the heart, add a frill, then draw a picture of his or her valentine on it. Now turn on the lights and display the pictures. Good for laughs any time.

GREAT LOVERS CHARADES

No fun-party is complete without a round or two of "the game." This version is to be acted out by couples.

Preliminary preparations: Slips containing the names of famous lovers have been placed in a bowl. A table nearby is supplied with props such as false mustaches, daggers, guns, tree branches, cardboard moon, paper roses, hats, capes, fans, a hobby horse, etc.

Assuming that we have twenty at a party, teams are made up of five couples to a side. Couples take turns, first one team and then the other, selecting a slip from the bowl. They get a quick look at it, then must immediately start acting without discussing it with one another. They perform for their own team to try to guess who they are. A limit of two minutes is given.

Suggestions:

Adam and Eve
Romeo and Juliet
Punch and Judy
Scarlett and Rhett Butler
Roy Rogers and Dale Evans.

HARLEQUIN MASK PATTERN

1. Cut masks from bright-colored art paper.
2. Across top of each, glue a row of sequins.
3. Brush bottom edge with glue, sprinkle thickly with multicolored glitter.

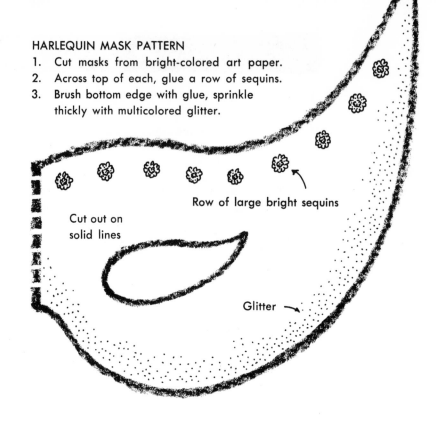

Row of large bright sequins

Cut out on solid lines

Glitter →

HARLEQUIN MASK STAND-UP PLACE CARD

1. Cut masks from bright-colored art paper.
2. Brush bottom edge with glue, sprinkle thickly with multicolored glitter.
3. Fold in center so that it will stand up.

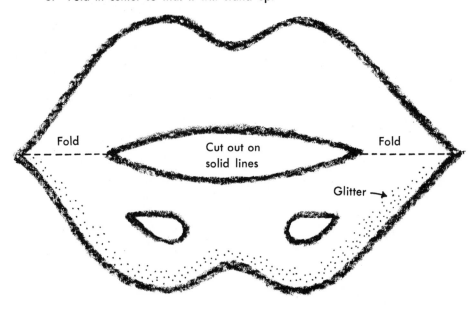

Fold

Cut out on solid lines

Fold

Glitter →

VALENTINE QUIZ

The answers to the questions below are words formed from letters found in the word "Valentines." Provide paper and pencils.

1. Time before Easter..............Lent
2. Roofing material................Tin
3. A number.......................Ten
4. Made by birds..................Nest
5. Public stopping place...........Inn
6. Used in fishing.................Net
7. Son of Jacob...................Levi
8. Opposite of good...............Evil
9. Small body of land.............Isle
10. A plant.......................Vine
11. False statement................Lie
12. River in Egypt.................Nile
13. A building spot................Site
14. To make fast..................Tie
15. Worn with a hat...............Veil
16. Part of a fork................Tine
17. Used on cuts and bruises........Salve
18. Stories ....Tales
19. Before ten....................Nine
20. Strong metal..................Steel

FAMOUS-LOVERS QUIZ

Girls make up one team, boys the other. They line up facing one another as in an old-fashioned spelling bee. I wonder which will know the most about romance?

Prior to the party, the chairman of the entertainment committee makes up a list of questions pertaining to great lovers. Include some about present-day lovers.

To start the quiz, she asks the captain of one team a question. If it is answered correctly, the next question is put to the captain of the other team. When a player misses a question, he is retired, and the same question is put to the next person in line on the opposite side.

Sample questions:

What two lovers do we think of in connection with a balcony?

What Egyptian princess loved what Roman emperor?

Our first President married what Virginia belle?

You go on from there. Make a pretty extensive list of questions, some difficult and some easy.

"I LOVE YOU" CUTOUT

teens' Broomstick party

The first crisp bite of autumn is in the air. The brightly colored hills, hazy with woodsmoke, remind us that Halloween is near, and that it is high time to start planning a party.

The invitation might read:

The wind is howling, and black is the night
Spooks are prowling, and black cats fight
Old witch in her cave will be out soon
Let's jump on her broomstick and ride to
the moon

ALL ABOARD!!!!

NOTICE Spooks, bring one pumpkin!
Witches, bring one broom!

There might be a little sketch here, showing jeans-clad teenagers riding the broom towards the moon. Their left hands are on the broom handle, their right hands are waving at you, all the mouths are wide open yelling, "Get Aboard!"

Sounds like fun, doesn't it?

184

PLANS IN BRIEF

Place. Any recreation room or good-sized living room. Of course, a cabin in the woods would be ideal.

Date. October 31st.

Time. 5:30 to 10:30 P.M.

Food. Wiener, corn, and potato bake.

Dress. Jeans.

Music. Record player . . . each guest brings favorite records . . . sweet as well as bop.

Number of Guests. Sixteen.

Entertainment. Games, Dances, Scavenger Hunt, Fireside Fun.

Price of admission. Spooks (boys) each bring a hollowed-out but uncarved pumpkin. Witches (girls) each bring a broomstick.

This party should be planned and carried out by the teenagers themselves. Mother should stay in the background.

EERIE ATMOSPHERE

Brightly colored leaves, real or artificial, and blue and green Christmas lights wired together, and tacked up over doorways, windows, mantels, etc. (Autumn leaves may be preserved indefinitely by dipping them in melted paraffin, then pressing them with a hot iron between two pieces of heavy brown paper. It preserves both their color and shape.)

Grinning jack-o-lanterns set on posts outside to greet the guests.

Black cats, made of construction paper, with green eyes, red mouth, red nostrils, pinned on the lamp shades. (These cats are very effective with their long whiskers. Orange bow ties may be pinned on some of them, and bewitching orange hair bows on others. Very decorative used as place mats at a sitdown supper. See "How-to" Section.)

False faces used two ways: Some pinned on lamp shades, and some tied on yardsticks and propped up outside so that they appear to be peeking in the windows.

Spider Web. See "Pre-supper High Jinks" for instructions.

Table decorations. To make cloth, buy six yards of orange cotton yard goods. Divide into two three-yard lengths and seam the edges together. Hem the ends of the cloth. This will cost you about $2.00 and will give you a cloth 72 by 108 inches, from which you can get years of wear. With this, use Halloween paper plates, mugs, and napkins. For the centerpiece, use a large plate on which are arranged candy apples, peppermint sticks in oranges, and marshmallows. These are reserved for later when all are gathered around the fireplace at the ghost-story session. Colored leaves and blue lights are arranged around the centerpiece, and if there is room, a jack-o-lantern can be placed at each end of the table. Black witch cutouts are pinned to cloth overhang.

(See page 190.)

Menu

Wiener, Corn, and Potato Bake

Toasted Buns

Celery and Carrot Sticks, Pickles

Doughnuts

**Hot Mulled Cider*

Candied Apples on a Stick

Peppermint Sticks in Oranges

Marshmallows

Starred items will be found in the recipe section.

RECIPES

WIENER, CORN, AND POTATO BAKE

Arrange in two roasting pans in oven or in
electric roaster:
   A layer of sweet potatoes
   A layer of white potatoes
   1 cup of water

Cover roaster and bake 30 minutes in 400-
degree oven. Add:
   A layer of corn-on-the-cob
   A layer of wieners

Continue baking, covered, for 30 minutes
longer.
Serve with plenty of butter.

HOT MULLED CIDER

Sixteen cups

1 gal. apple cider
6 sticks cinnamon
1 tbsp. whole cloves

1 tbsp. allspice
2 pieces whole mace
2 cups brown sugar

Tie spices in bag. Stir in sugar. Simmer for
15 to 20 minutes covered. Remove spices.
Serve hot, with a stick of cinnamon in each
mug.

PEPPERMINT STICKS IN ORANGES

Select 16 uniform navel oranges. Insert apple corer ¾ of the way through each orange. Place a peppermint stick in the hole. It should fit snugly. The stick serves as a straw, and by squeezing the orange, the juice may be drawn up. The flavor is really special!

A JOB FOR EACH

Everyone helps prepare supper, and that is part of the fun. Make a list of jobs to do, and have each guest draw one.

After school on the party day let one couple make Mulled Cider; core the oranges; prepare celery and carrot sticks and refrigerate.

At partytime, the first couple to arrive starts the wiener bake, and butters buns for toasting in broiler or fireplace.

PRE-SUPPER HIGH JINKS

Halloween party fun depends largely on games and novelty dances. We hope you'll enjoy these.

SPIDER WEB

This is an oldie but still fun and a wonderful ice-breaker. It also acts as colorful decoration, and sets a party mood from the time you set foot in the door.

You are met by a regular network of yarn in every conceivable color, which has been wound around tables, under rugs and in and among other pieces of yarn. Each person is given a clothespin attached to a piece of yarn, and the winner will be the first one to reach the ugly spider suspended from the ceiling. A squeeze bulb has secretly been attached to the spider, which leaps down just as the winner reaches for it. Shrieks!! Or, if you prefer, fortunes may be attached to ends of yarn.

FORTUNES

For the girls

You'll have offers of marriage from men of renown
And riches and jewels and objects of art
This means nothing to you, you'll turn them all down
And marry a man with a loving heart

For the boys

The black cat tells me your luck is unbelievable
Your luck is fantastic, it's almost inconceivable
Your wife will be a beauty with figure divine
She can cook and can sew and owns a gold mine.

For the girls

The cards have just said that at twenty you'll
    wed
There'll be room in your cottage for two
But when twins come along, then triplets,
    then quads,
Then what are you going to do?

You'll meet a man on one of your tours
You lucky girl, his love is all yours
You'll live in the lap of luxury
As an old man's darling, wait and see.

You'll be unmarried at 25
Your friends will fear you'll be a spinster
You'll fall in love at 26
And wed the handsome minister.

To wed a wise man is your fate
He may look tame but oh you wait.

You'll travel in Michigan, Kansas and Maine
With pleasure your days will be rife
'Neath Florida's palms you'll meet a bold
    swain
Who'll persuade you to try wedded life.

A movie star you'll surely be
Courted and wooed in every land
But the one who will win you will be your
    old beau
Who's content to hold your hand.

My witch's brew shows this for you
A husband dark and tall
A handsome face, a summer place,
My dear, you'll have a ball.

Five or six children for you I see
Or is it nine or ten? Dear me . . .

I see in my cauldron by the light of the moon
A fair-haired stranger, you'll wed in June.

For the boys

I see in you the makings of a military man
Your shoes are brightly polished, and you're
    always spic and span
You'll surely be a Captain on the high high
    sea
Or even an Admiral in the great Nav-ee.

You'll dig for priceless treasure
Like Captain Kidd of old
Uranium the object of your search
Instead of jewels and gold.

The spirits advise me you're now rough and
    wild
But as a husband you'll be meek and mild.

My powers on earth are quite supernatural
But my forecasts you'll find are always quite
    factual
Your wives I see, number three.

Your wife? an ex-lion tamer
A veritable shrew
And she'll use her talents
To tame little you.

A doctor or lawyer, I can't tell which
But that's pretty close for a poor old witch
Beware—a dark woman appears in the night
She's pretty until—you turn on the light.

A dancer you'll be
You'll twist and twirl
But never will find
Your ideal girl.

JACK-O-LANTERN CONTEST

A hollowed-out pumpkin is given to each couple. Together they design the jack-o-lantern and secure and light the candle.

Give blue ribbons for the best, and the worst!

WITCHIE

Have the artist in your group paint a five-foot witch on an old sheet with textile paints. Leave an opening where the face should be. Attach black yarn for the hair. Hang the sheet in a doorway.

Each boy in turn sticks his head through the opening, making as horrible a face as possible.

Have a flash camera handy for this one—a photographer's dream.

SCAVENGER HUNT

By the light of the moon on Halloween—what better time for a good old-fashioned scavenger hunt!

Each couple is given a list of articles to find and bring within 30 minutes.

Suggestions: old broom, corn candy, black mask, cobweb, bone, orange candle, skull-and-crossbones label.

BALLOON-SWEEPING RELAY

You will need for each girl:

1 broom
1 balloon (each one a different color)

Girls line up on one side of the room, boys on the other. Balloons are placed on starting line. At the signal each girl sweeps the balloon across to her partner. He quickly grabs broom and sweeps the balloon back to other side. First couple through wins.

CHOOSE YOUR PARTNER

FARMYARD PARTNERS

Each girl draws a slip on which is written the name of an animal. Give duplicate slips to the boys. At the signal, each player starts imitating his animal until he finds his mate, who will be making similar calls.

Familiar ones: cow, pig, dog, cat, donkey, horse, duck, turkey, rooster, wolf, sheep, hen, turtle dove, crow, chick, mouse.

BALLOON SCRAMBLE

Each girl is given a blown-up balloon which has a slip inside containing her name. The girls form a circle inside and dance to the right. The boys form a circle outside and dance to the left. At the signal, girls bat balloons high in the air. The boys scramble for them, and have to break the balloons to find their partners' names.

BACKWARD BUMP

Girls and boys line up at opposite sides of the room facing the wall. As the record starts, all start walking backwards—no peek-in'. The one you bump into is your partner.

WITCH PATTERN
Cut out on solid lines

POST-SUPPER DANCING

MULTIPLICATION DANCE

One couple starts dancing. The music stops. They separate and each chooses a new partner. Continue until all are dancing.

THE ORANGE DANCE

Each couple places an orange between their foreheads, and begins dancing. The couple who keeps it there longest wins.

FOLLOW THE LEADER

Couples line up behind the leaders. Whatever they do, the rest must follow.
Here are some suggestions:

1. Form a conga line, and zig-zag back and forth.
2. Couples stand side by side and skate across the floor.
3. Two couples, put their arms around each other, and dance together.
4. Do the elephant walk. Form a single line and walk on all fours.

When you have an extra boy or girl

THE SKELETON DANCE

Prior to the party, paint a cardboard skeleton with luminous paint. The extra guest dances with the skeleton. Lights are turned off, and the extra person tries to tap someone on the back with the skeleton. Then that person must dance with IT. Everyone tries to avoid getting near the thing, glowing spookily in the dark.

FIRESIDE FUN

By this time everyone is glad to flop down in front of the fire and rest. Also, everyone is hungry again, so now is the time to bring out the popcorn, candied apples, marshmallows, peppermint sticks in oranges, and anything else that is lying around. We hope that you have thought to have the boys whittle long pointed sticks on which to toast the marshmallows.

Now is the time for your ghost-story scripts, and "Continued Ghost Story" so gather your props together, but keep them hidden until time to use them.

GHOST-STORY SCRIPT

Prior to the party, ask guests to form teams of four or eight. Each team is to prepare a ghost-story script which is to be performed the night of the party. If it is too much trouble to memorize it, the script may be read by the light of the flickering flames. The main thing is to put plenty of expression in the reading, and to have plenty of

sound effects, such as groans, whistles, screams, etc. Tapping the window pane, and flashing lights from outside the windows give fine eerie effects. A nice gruesome effect is achieved when a face appears at the window. This can be done by securing an ugly mask to a yardstick and moving it to and fro. Each play should run about four minutes.

CONTINUED GHOST STORY

The Head Spook starts a ghost story. At an exciting stage he throws a white fur mouse at one of the guests. This is the signal for that person to continue the story, and so it goes. Here is a sample:

"Fiercely the storm raged, the rain came down in torrents, and the wind whistled like a mad thing. The two girls had become lost in the storm, and had unwittingly stumbled into the old haunted house for shelter. The shutters banged, the wind shrieked through the panes of broken glass. They crept up the stairs to try to find a dryer spot. At the head of the stairs they froze in terror. What was that??? A heavy thumping

noise came up the dark stairway. It's on the first stair . . . It's on the second stair . . . It's on the top stair . . . It's coming toward you . . . It's . . . . . ."

At this point the Head Spook throws the white mouse to someone who takes up the story from there. At the end of ten or fifteen minutes, the Head Spook calls time, and finishes the story with something like this:

"The thing is coming closer . . . It's outside the cabin . . . It's coming through the door . . . It's getting nearer . . . . . . It's . . . got you!

(At this point, leap into the air and yell at the top of your lungs.)

"HOW-TO" SECTION

BLACK CATS

You will need:

For each cat, a piece of black art paper, 12 by 18 inches.
1 sheet of shiny green paper.
1 sheet of shiny red paper.
Pieces of 2-inch-square white paper.

Trace around pattern, extending whiskers so that they measure about 6 inches long. Bring each one to a point at end.

To make eyes: Cut circles from the green paper about the size of a 25-cent piece. Paste one in the center of each piece of white paper. Tape to the back so that the green eyes show through the eyeholes.

Red mouth and nostrils: Cut squares of shiny red paper about 4 inches square. Tape to the back. Red shows through for nostrils and mouth.

Use black cats as place mats, pin on lamp shades, use as wall decorations. Make good take-home favors for children.

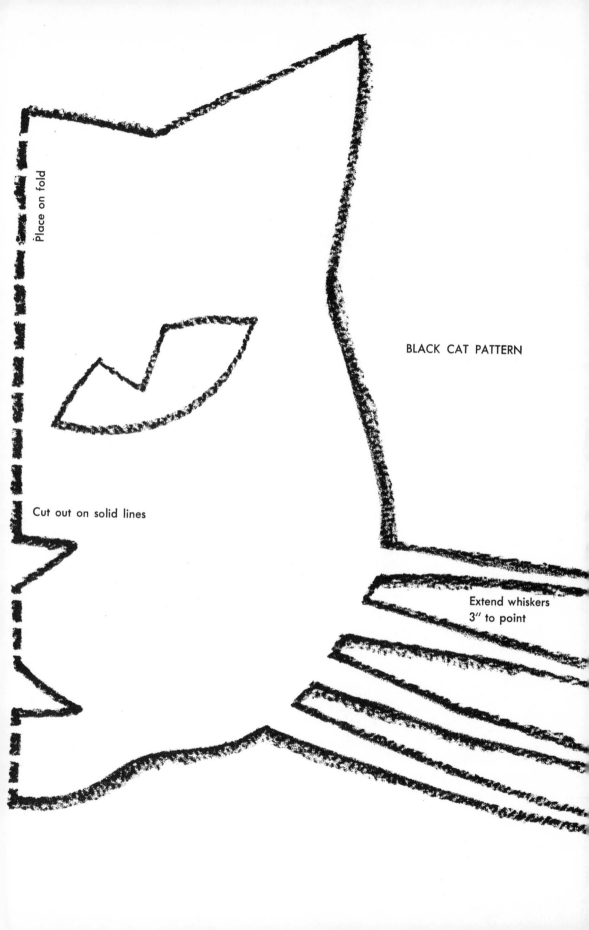

Place on fold

Cut out on solid lines

BLACK CAT PATTERN

Extend whiskers
3" to point

randy's Chuck Wagon party

"Ride 'em Cowboy. Let 'er buck. *Whoa!*"— a common expression heard in Calgary, Alberta, Canada, during the world-famous Stampede Week each year in July.

Cowboys come from all parts of Canada, the United States, and Mexico to compete for the World Championship Bucking Bronco title. There are Indians' bareback pony races, calf-roping contests, Mounties' cavalry drills, and other wonderful events.

However, none of these attractions can compare with the thrill of the Chuck-wagon Races. These are held each evening about 7:30 in front of the grandstand, and are the most colorful and exciting events to watch that you can imagine. Each of these chuck-wagon outfits is owned by a different ranch, which is one reason that the competition is so keen. You'll notice the brand of each outfit painted on the side of the chuck wagon. Many times all the cowboys in an outfit have on shirts and neckerchiefs in the same bright color.

The scene just before the race is a peaceful one. The cowboys are sitting around the stove in front of the chuck wagon just finishing a leisurely supper. Horses are grazing contentedly nearby.

At the signal, however, bedlam breaks loose. The stove, dishes, pots and pans are all thrown into the chuck wagon; horses are caught; four are harnessed to the chuck wagon, four are saddled and mounted by outriders, and they're off in a tremendous cloud of dust—all in a matter of seconds. First they make a figure 8 around two barrels

in the infield, then off they go racing around the track, chuck wagons leaning precariously on the curves.

Can't you just see them coming down the stretch, horses flying, chuck wagons swaying from side to side, stove and pots and pans rattling around in the wagon, riders pounding along beside it yelling encouragement to their driver, and the spectators in the grandstand going wild? Once seen, never forgotten.

WILD WEST ATMOSPHERE

BRANDS

JV Half
Diamond

Double U

Lazy T

Arrow

Diamond A

Bar C

Circle I

HK

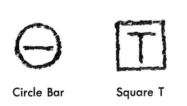

Circle Bar

Square T

Now, it isn't possible for all of you to participate in a chuck-wagon race, but you *can* give a chuck-wagon party in the wide open spaces of your own back yard. Here's how.

For wild-West atmosphere, draw brands on 9-inch squares of colored art paper with black paint. Tack brands up on a fence.

Also make signs saying: CALGARY STAMPEDE, PENDLETON ROUNDUP, etc., to tack up on trees.

FOR YOUR "CHUCK-WAGON" TABLE

Lay planks across two sawhorses. Secure three heavy wires or hoops about 1 inch apart to sides of planks on back ends of table, and cover with gunny sacking. This forms the canopy. Add wheels if desired. Nail kegs from a hardware supply house topped by round brown cushions serve as seats.

Red bandanas are used for napkins. Use tin pie plates, tin cups, salts and peppers. Red kerosene lanterns and field flowers in a ketchup bottle add color. Favors are cowboy neckerchiefs and magnets in the shape of horseshoes.

Of course, you all wear your Western garb and tote your six-shooters.

INVITATIONS

The invitations are easy to make if you follow these patterns and directions:

You will need:

Tan art paper 9 by 12 inches. One piece will make two invitations.
Dark brown crayon.
White writing paper.

1. Fold art paper in half so that it will measure 6 by 9 inches.
2. Place pattern on the art paper so that the back part of wagon is on fold.
3. Trace with pencil, then cut out. Do not cut the section on the fold. This holds it together. Do not cut out the round section.
4. Draw in wheels as in illustration with brown crayon.
5. Write invitation on white paper and staple it inside.
6. Cut wagon top of white writing paper. Fill in curved lines as in illustration with brown crayon. Cut out the round section for the opening.
7. Paste white section on top to fit.

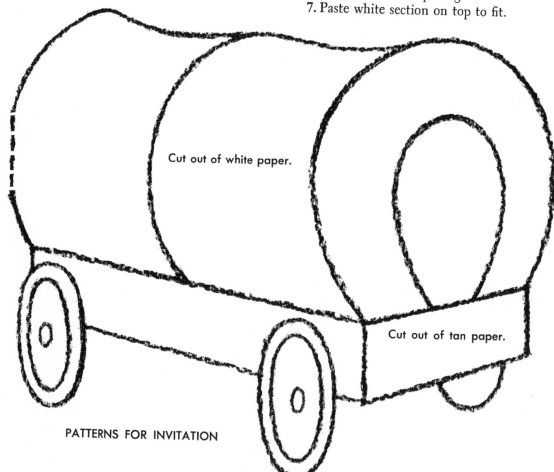

Cut out of white paper.

Cut out of tan paper.

PATTERNS FOR INVITATION

The invitation reads:

Oh say, Roy Rogers,
And you, Daniel Boone,
There's a chuck-wagon party
That's a-comin' pretty soon.
The good guys and the bad guys
Are a-headin' this way, so
Bring yer shootin' irons, pardner,
Saddle up—Let's go!
Saturday, October 8, from 6 to 8
At Dry Gulch Ranch, otherwise known as
Randy Mains' house, Northridge, Calif.

COME AND GET IT

Try cooking your own chow outdoors over an open fire or grill.

A typical cowboy meal out on the range at roundup time might be:

> Steak   Baked Spuds   Buns
>
> Canned Peas or Corn
>
> Apple Pie   Cocoa

Cube steaks sprinkled with meat tenderizer several hours ahead are wonderfully tasty, and cost little if any more than hamburgers. Grill them 2 to 3 minutes per side. They cook very quickly. Maybe Mother or Dad could give you a hand with these.

Bake the potatoes on top of grill 45 minutes before putting on the steaks. If they are wrapped securely in foil, there will be no danger of burning, and they will keep hot while you are broiling your steaks. Guests serve themselves, then get their steaks sizzling hot off the fire. Have ketchup and steak sauce nearby.

STEER-ROPIN' CONTEST

On a piece of plywood or scrap lumber, paint the head of a long-horned steer. Pound several spikes into the horns. Each contestant has 3 tries to rope the steer with rope quoits or a lariat.

SHOOTIN' CONTEST

Tack a target up on a fence. Let each player have three shots at it with a toy gun that shoots harmless, yet accurate, cork pellets, available through mail-order catalogues.

THE CHASE

This is an obstacle race. Before the party, print the eight signs below; set them up around the yard as indicated. Each sign represents a certain spot in the yard, and tells the players what to do:

Phantom Corral .....“Start Here”
    (at starting line)
Hangman's Tree......“Run Around Tree”
    (pole in ground)
Water Hole..........“Take Drink”
    (pail of water, paper cups)
Ambush Tunnel......“Crawl Through”
    (three overturned chairs)

Shady Canyon........"Take Nap"
    (any shady spot)
Sheer Cliff..........."Turn Somersault"
    (small pile of sand)
Snake Lake.........."Jump Across"
    (tub of water)
Desperado Hideaway.."Get in and Roll"
    (barrel open at ends)

At partytime, divide guests into two teams—Good Guys and Bad Guys. At a signal, the first player on each team races through the obstacle course and back to the starting line, where he touches the next player, who then does the same, etc., until all players have participated.

RANCH-LIFE QUIZ BEE

Ahead of time, prepare a list of questions about cowboys and ranch life, a different question for each guest. Here are some samples you could use:

What is a chuck wagon?
The wagon from which cowboys have their meals when out on the range.
What is a ten-gallon hat?
A wide-brimmed cowboy hat.
How do cattlemen identify their cattle?
By the brands.

What is the name of Roy Rogers' horse?
Trigger.
What used to be the penalty for stealing a horse?
Hanging.
Name three states where you'll find many cowboys.
Texas, Arizona, Nevada.

When ready, divide guests into two teams; have them sit on the ground facing each other. Ask questions first of one team, then the other. When a player fails to answer correctly, he drops out.

STAGECOACH

Before the party, write a wild-West story depicting the holdup of a stagecoach. Mention these characters frequently: cowboy, young lady schoolteacher, driver, guard, sheriff, outlaw, etc.

At partytime, appoint one child to be the narrator, and the other children to act the characters in the story. The children sit on the nail kegs, and the narrator reads the story aloud. As each character is mentioned, the child who represents that character runs around his nail keg and sits down again. Whenever the narrator says, "stagecoach," the children change places; in the confusion, the narrator tries to get one of the other places. If he succeeds, he becomes one of the characters and the player who lost his place becomes narrator.

SING-SONG

Cowboys love to sit around a campfire in the evening after supper singing Western ballads. You should all know the words of these old favorites: "Home on the Range," "Red River Valley," "You Are My Sunshine," "Top of Old Baldy," "She'll Be Comin' Round the Mountain."

ALTERNATE

After supper has been served, all the pirates sit around the deck to "swap yarns."

One pirate starts telling of one of his dastardly deeds. He builds it up to a point where the suspense is terrific, then points his dagger at another pirate, who carries on from there. And so on until each pirate has had an opportunity to add to the yarn.

Menu

* Franks à la Buccaneer

Toasted Frankfurter Rolls

Mixed Green Salad

* "Pirate-Ship" Cake Sticks   Ice cream

Hot Chocolate

* Starred items will be found in recipe section.

RECIPES

FRANKS À LA BUCCANEER

You will need per person:

1 frankfurter	1 slice bacon
1 slice cheese, 3 by 1	Easy Bar B-Q Sauce
by ¼ inches	1 frankfurter roll
1 sliver sweet pickle	
Prepared mustard	
(optional)	

Easy Bar B-Q Sauce

1 cup Heinz chili sauce
1 tbsp. maple syrup
2 tbsp. Worcestershire sauce

Slice frank almost through lengthwise.
Place piece of cheese the length of the frank.
  Add mustard if desired.
Place pickle on the cheese.
Wrap the frank in a piece of bacon. Secure
  with toothpicks.
Broil until bacon is crisp.
Place franks in frying pan, and simmer 5
  minutes in Easy Bar B-Q Sauce. Place each
  frank in a toasted buttered frankfurter
  bun. Eat while hot.

"PIRATE-SHIP" CAKE STICKS

You will need:

1 pkg. prepared chocolate cake mix
1 cornstick pan
1 pkg. chocolate frosting mix
White paper sails (see pattern below)

Make up the chocolate cake according to directions on the package.

Grease cornstick pan generously.

Spoon batter into sections of pan until each one is half filled. Bake.

Cool cakes before removing from pan. Make slit lengthwise in the top of each cake. Ice with chocolate frosting. Insert sail.

A row of these down the center of the table would be effective.

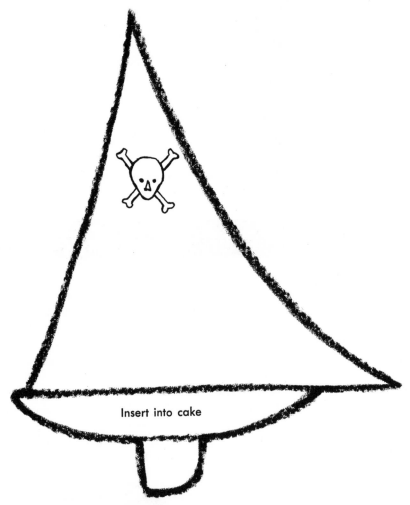

Insert into cake

PATTERN FOR SAILS FOR PIRATE SHIP CUPCAKES
Cut sail from lightweight white cardboard or construction paper. Draw skull and crossbones with India ink.

SHOPPING LISTS

Grocery list *

For the franks you will need per person:

1 frankfurter
1 slice cheese 3 by 1 inches
1 sliver sweet pickle
1 slice bacon
1 frankfurter roll
  Other groceries:
Salad greens and dressing
1 pkg. chocolate cake mix
1 pkg. chocolate frosting mix
Ice cream

Miscellaneous list

Colored construction paper for invitations,
  favors, and decorations
1 green light bulb
1 red light bulb
A wooden treasure chest from dime 'store
Red candles
Gold-foil-wrapped candy
Balloons
Envelopes for invitations

* Does not include staples.

SERVICE

1. Place one frankfurter on bun on each plate at table.
2. Fill mugs with hot chocolate.
3. Call guests to supper.
4. Pass salad in a bowl.
5. When guests have finished main course, remove plates to kitchen.
6. Bring in the ice cream on a dessert plate.
7. Invite guests to each have a "Pirate Ship" cupcake. (These had been arranged in a row down the center of the table before guests arrived.)
8. Offer seconds on the hot chocolate.

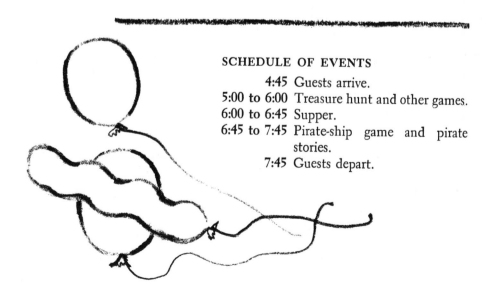

SCHEDULE OF EVENTS

4:45 Guests arrive.
5:00 to 6:00 Treasure hunt and other games.
6:00 to 6:45 Supper.
6:45 to 7:45 Pirate-ship game and pirate stories.
7:45 Guests depart.

"HOW-TO" SECTION

INVITATIONS

How to make:

Cut a piece of black construction paper, 3½ by 12 inches.

Cut a piece of heavy white writing paper, 3 by 10½ inches. Fold each piece in half.

On the left side of the writing paper, print the details of the party, such as:

> A ghastly crew of pirates most bold,
> Will sail seeking treasure of jewelry and gold.
> All hands on deck at a quarter to five.
> Ahoy there, Matey, Look alive!
> The schooner won't wait, so don't be late.
> We dock again at quarter to eight!
>
> (For secret password, hold this invitation up to the light)

On the right side print:

> Bobby Foster's Birthday Party
> 120 Valley Avenue
> Blue Mountain, California
> Friday, October 14

Now place the white paper at the top of the black paper, so that the white paper is just a little below the top edge of the black. Fold together and staple through all four thicknesses of paper.

Turn to the inside again, and on the black part at the bottom, print in large letters, PIRATE SHIP. Then take a pin, and make small holes at intervals on the inside page where you have printed. In this way, the secret password will show up plainly when you hold it up to the light.

For the cover of the invitation. First draw a curving line from the left side to the right side as illustrated below.

Then cut out small pennants from construction paper—red, white, blue, yellow, green, etc. Make some square, some triangular, some in rectangles. Paste these along the white line, like pennants on a ship. (*Note:* This invitation will fit regular-size envelopes.)

HOW TO MAKE PENNANTS FOR ROOM DECORATIONS

Using either construction paper or remnants of bright cloth, cut out pennants in various shapes, about 12 inches in width. Staple or pin them to a piece of tape. Attach one end to a high spot in the room. Attach the other to a low spot in the room.

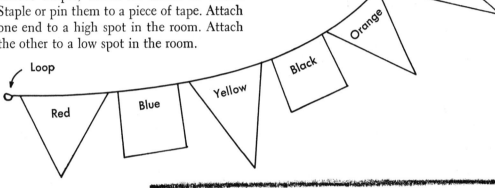

HOW TO MAKE PIRATE-SHIP CENTERPIECE

Sailboats may-be bought in variety stores for about $2.00 or you may have an old one on hand. These usually have plastic sails with designs on them that would be unsuitable for a pirate ship. Leaving the masts and lines intact, cut away the plastic sails. Replace them with sails made of stiff white paper. Glue them with cement glue to the masts.

From thin white cardboard, cut 5- by 8-inch place cards. Fold in half so that they will stand up. On each, outline a Jolly Roger insignia, with top of insignia at fold. Cut out around top of insignia as shown. Write name of pirate on each. Some suggestions: Captain Kidd, Jean Lafitte, Captain Morgan, Long John Silver, etc.

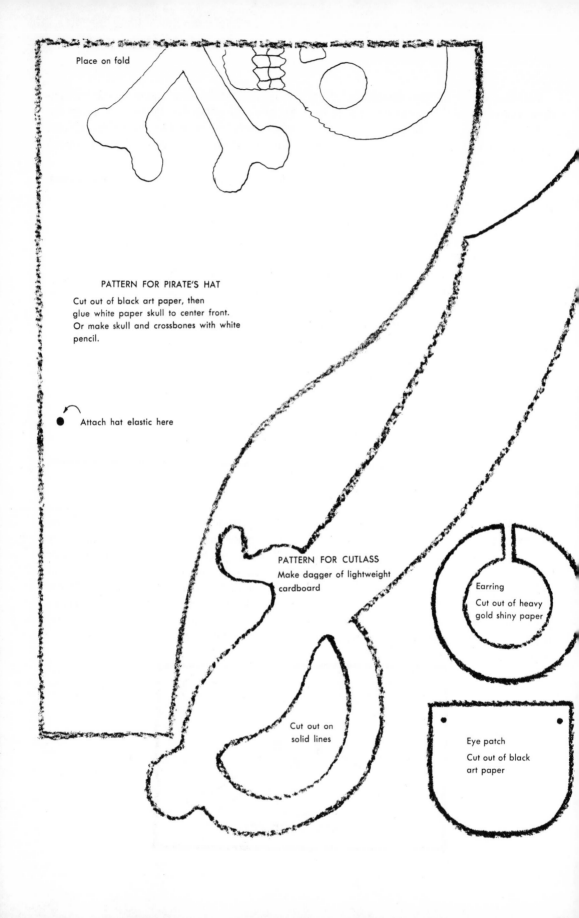

Place on fold

PATTERN FOR PIRATE'S HAT

Cut out of black art paper, then
glue white paper skull to center front.
Or make skull and crossbones with white
pencil.

Attach hat elastic here

PATTERN FOR CUTLASS
Make dagger of lightweight
cardboard

Cut out on
solid lines

Earring

Cut out of heavy
gold shiny paper

Eye patch

Cut out of black
art paper

nancy's Circus party

Just the very word "circus" brings spine-tingling memories of stirring circus band music, the gigantic glittering parade, the elephants in their spangly trappings, the trained lions and tigers, the trapeze performers.

Circus parties are as much fun in the fall and winter as at any other time. The decorations, food, and general carnival spirit seem to recapture some of the magic of summertime. But then, circus parties are always fun. I can't imagine there being a dull one, can you?

This one is designed to please the four to seven set so,

> *"Start the circus music, Joe,*
> *Take the tickets, and off we go."*

EXCITING INVITATIONS

Many attractive invitations with a circus motif may be bought in stationery and ten-cent stores, but since half the fun of a party is preparing for it, we like to make our own.

This one is a red and white circus tent. When you peek inside the tent you will read:

Circus Party at Nancy's
Hark, Hark, the dogs do bark
The Circus is coming to town.
Your admission is paid,
There's pink lemonade,
A merry-go-round and a clown.
Please reply   *Fri. Oct. 7 3.30-5.30*

Directions for making circus tent:
1. Cut pattern #1 out of white writing paper.
2. Cut pattern #2 out of red construction paper. Paste to white paper at top.
3. Write or print invitation with red pencil.
4. Cut pattern #3 twice out of red construction paper. Staple to white paper at sides.

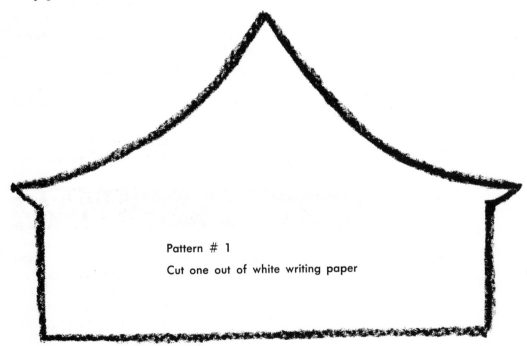

Pattern # 1

Cut one out of white writing paper

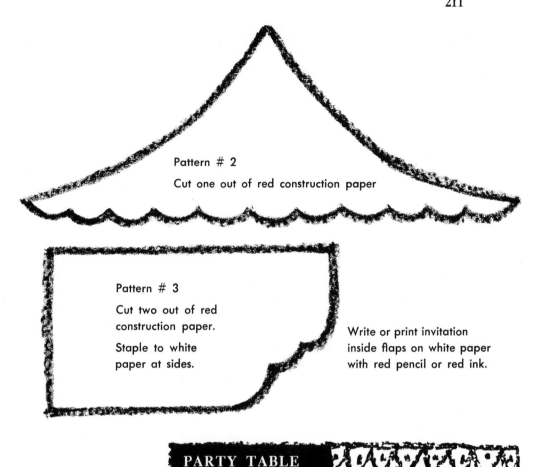

Pattern # 2

Cut one out of red construction paper

Pattern # 3

Cut two out of red construction paper.

Staple to white paper at sides.

Write or print invitation inside flaps on white paper with red pencil or red ink.

PARTY TABLE

Children's eyes will light up like skyrockets when they see this gaily set table.

TABLE. Extenda-top (round) table over bridge table.

CLOTHS. 81-inch round white cloth (made from old sheet), 72-inch round red cloth, made from 4 yards percale rounded, then scalloped around edges to resemble circus tent. Place red cloth over the white.

NAPKINS. Heavy, embossed-type paper napkins, white.

CHINA. White paper plates, smooth embossed type, good quality.

SILVER. Plastic forks and iced teaspoons, varicolored.

GLASSWARE. Tall, clear ten-cent glasses, with pipe cleaner clowns attached to top.

CENTERPIECE. Merry-go-round set on revolving happy-birthday cake plate–music box. A gay pennant flies from top of merry-go-round. Merry-go-round is encircled by tiny flowerpots painted red. So that the flowerpots will hold water, melt down some old candles, cover hole in bottom of pot with tape, pour an inch of melted wax in bottom of pot. Let harden.

CANDLES. Red votive around flowerpots.

PLACE CARDS. Rubber circus animals have mouths which open. A piece of colored yarn leads from their mouths to place cards, on which are rhymes. (Animals cost ten cents.)

THE TENT. Red crepe-paper streamers hang from doorway to the floor. The center ones are then draped back and pinned to make a tent-like entrance.

MUSIC. Records of stirring circus music and marches are available and add a lot to the circus atmosphere.

FAVORS. Clown hats, clown ruffs, clown masks.

FAVORS

To make clown hats

Make each one a different color

Use a piece of construction paper 12 by 12 inches.

Join two corners with a curved line. (Place the ruler in one corner, and measure down 12 inches as you swing across. Make two or three marks as a guide.)

Cut on curved line.

Carefully fold one edge over the other, and secure with a staple.

With colored Mystik tape, cover the seam from top to bottom. You now have a cone-shaped hat.

Attach varicolored pompons down center of seam.

Attach hat elastics.

To make pompons

Have Nancy hold up two fingers about 2 inches apart. Wind colored yarn around and around her fingers, about ten times. Tie in the center tightly, then slip off. Cut the loops and there is your pompon. I like the yarn that goes from one color into another in shades of green, yellow, orange, red, blue, etc.

To make ruff

Use crepe paper. Leave folded. Cut a strip 2 inches wide. Ruffle it on the sewing machine using #6 position. This will make about four ruffs.

To make masks

Use 9- by 12-inch construction paper. Draw clown mask in pencil, then cut out eyes, ears, mouth. Attach yarn tie backs or hat elastics. If desired, masks may be decorated with sequins.

PLACE CARD RHYMES

I'm a little fat elephant
With floppy pink ears.
If you don't sit here, Tommy,
I'll break into tears.

I'm a precious little panda
From far across the sea.
Barbara, I'm lonesome!
Please sit in front of me.

I'm a ferocious lion
But there's nothing to fear,
For I like Susie
She can sit right here.

I'm a little brown bear
I'm cute and smart too!
You're my favorite, Bobby,
And I've saved this spot for you.

I'm a trained dog
I do tricks, quite a few.
Sally, you sit here
And I'll wave my tongue at you.

I've saved this place for Dennis
Sit right here, please do;
We have lots in common
For I'm a monkey, too!

Of course you substitute the names of your
own cherubs.

CIRCUS DECORATIONS

Two toy clowns sit on edge of a table with their feet hanging down over the edge. A gaily striped umbrella is secured in sand in a flowerpot, and is open over them.

Red and white streamers may be secured to a ceiling fixture, draped to the tops of windows, and allowed to fall gracefully to the floor.

Sheets pinned together and placed over a clothesline or heavy cord which has been secured at each side of room makes a fine tent for playing games. Bricks or other heavy articles may be used to tie down sheet.

Cut out pictures of circus animals and tack up around room.

Menu

Open-faced Tuna Sandwiches

Pink Lemonade

* Clown Cookies

Strawberry Ice Cream Cones

Small children are usually too excited at a party to eat very much. I believe one piece of fresh sandwich bread with crusts removed will be enough for each child. Spread with tuna mixture, then cut in four pieces for easier handling.

Add a few drops of red coloring to your pitcher of lemonade. The frozen kind is very good. An ice cube in which a maraschino cherry has been frozen adds a nice glamour touch.

RECIPE

CLOWN COOKIES

½ lb. margarine softened a little
¾ cup sugar
½ egg, beaten a little
½ tsp. baking powder
1 tsp. peppermint flavoring
3 cups sifted all-purpose flour

Cream the margarine and sugar.
Add the egg.
Add the baking powder and flavoring.
Beat well.
Add the flour.
Beat until smooth.
Flour your hands, and work the dough a little as if you were kneading it. Divide into four portions for easier handling.
Roll out on floured board about ¼ inch thick.

For clown head. Cut circles with a small biscuit cutter.

For clown hat. Cut triangle or cone shape and place immediately adjacent to the circle so that hat will fit head (see drawing).

For bow. Make a strip of dough 12 inches long by ¼ inch wide. Make a "figure 8" of it. Attach under clown's chin. (All three sections fit closely together, and they will join during the baking.)

Features

Cut a three-cornered purple gumdrop in two. Use one half for each eye. Use the curved section of a jellied orange slice for mouth and bake at 350 degrees 12 to 15 minutes until lightly browned.

Optional. Bake the head, hat, and bow separately. Frost the head with pink icing; frost the clown hat with chocolate icing; frost the bow with green icing. Then "glue" together with icing. Add the features with a decorating tube or with gumdrops as described. This method is more work, but very pretty and good to eat.

GROCERY LIST *

Tuna	Several gumdrops	Frozen lemonade	Strawberry ice cream
Fresh sandwich loaf	Several jellied orange	Maraschino cherries	Ice cream cones
Salad dressing	slices (or raspberry)	* Does not include staples.	

LET'S PLAY GAMES

THE BAG BLOW

To start the party off with a bang!

For six players: Place two chairs on one side of the room with three paper bags in each. The first member of each team dashes to the chair, takes a bag, blows it up, breaks it, and races back to touch the next in line. Each member of winning team gets a sucker.

THE HUNGRY CLOWN

A candy kiss toss

To make clown: Cover the outside of a carton (about 24 inches square and 24 inches deep) with white shelf paper. On one side draw a large clown. Paint in bright colors with poster paint. Cut out the mouth. Prop up the front of box a bit, so that it is easier for the children to throw in the kisses.

Each child is given six candy kisses. Score is kept, and the one who throws the greatest number into the clown's mouth gets first choice of the prizes on the table. Second place gets second choice, etc.

THE TICKING ALLIGATOR

Do you remember the alligator in Peter Pan who warned everyone of his approach by the loud ticking noise he made? Let's play a game using that idea.

Appoint someone to be the alligator. Give him a clock with a good loud tick, or a kitchen timer. All the children including the alligator are blindfolded. The alligator tries to catch someone, but this is fairly hard to do as the ticking noise warns them. If he does catch someone, that player becomes the alligator.

Plenty of suspense and squeals in this one.

ELEPHANT RACE

This race will not break any speed records, but is fun to do and fun to watch.

Children line up at the starting point. At the signal, they race toward the finish line on their hands and feet. Anyone who drops to his knees is out. Winner gets first choice at the prize table, then the others make their selections. It is wise to have several identical articles.

CIRCUS QUIZ BEE

Divide players into two teams facing one another. Mother or other adult prepares a list of approximately a hundred questions prior to the party, asks the questions, and acts as moderator.

Examples:

What animal is known as "king of the jungle"?	The Lion
What animal has the longest neck?	The Giraffe
Which animals act the most like human beings?	Monkeys, Apes, etc.
What is stretched underneath the trapeze in case a performer falls?	A net
What material is on the floor of the rings?	Sawdust
What is the man called who announces the acts?	Ringmaster
What is the large tent called in which the circus is performed?	Big Top
What is the largest circus on earth?	Ringling Bros. Barnum and Bailey
Which are the largest animals in a circus?	Elephants

This will give you an idea.

First the moderator asks a question of the captain of the first team. If he answers correctly then the second question goes to the captain of the second team. If a player misses a question, he drops out of the game, and the question goes to the other side. Player who stays in last gets first choice of prizes; the members of the winning team get second choice; members of the losing team all get a prize, too.

WHAT'S MY LINE?

Divide players into two teams. Each group represents people or animals who perform in a circus ring. The first team goes into a huddle, and decides what they are going to do. Then the ringmaster of ring number one says, "Here are the performers of ring number one."

Ringmaster number two says, "What can they do?"

Whereupon all the members of ring number one begin acting out their routines. If the second team guesses, they are allowed to perform. If not, the first team performs again.

Suggestions: Tightrope walkers, lion tamers, performing seals, trapeze performers, clowns, bareback riders.

PRIZES

In the four to seven age group, it might be better to give a small prize to each child rather than a more expensive prize to the winner. One fascinating way is to have a variety of penny or five-cent items displayed on a table. Winner gets first choice, then each of the others selects a prize. Or you may prefer to award each child a balloon, lollipop, toy horn, etc.

To save confusion, provide a small paper bag or other container in which each child may carry home his loot.

STORY-TIME

For a quiet interval before supper, seat all of your little guests in a circle, and have an older child or adult read them a circus story. If there is still time left, ask each one to tell which circus act he likes best.

SCHEDULE

3:30 Children arrive. Mother and Nancy welcome guests at the door. Nancy shows them where to put hats and coats. As children take off their wraps, Nancy gives each one a clown hat, ruff, and clown mask.

3:45 to 4:45 Games.

4:45 to 5:15 Supper.

5:15 to 5:30 Favors and prizes and wraps are gathered together and put in one place so that mothers may pick the children up without too much confusion.

As children thank Nancy and her mother for the party, Nancy says "Thank you for coming."

Mother goose party for tots

Sugar and spice and everything nice, that's what little girls are made of. This is our "pretty party" and is for tiny misses between the ages of four and seven.

Little ones love the familiar, so we decided to plan a party using the Mother Goose theme.

Mother Goose and her nursery rhyme characters are born anew with each generation. Who can forget the wide-eyed wonder· of a little child hearing for the first time of the cow who jumped over the moon, of the Old Woman in the Shoe, or of Little Jack Horner and his wondrous Christmas pie?

INVITATIONS

Here's something different in the way of invitations: For each child, blow up three balloons in pastel colors. With poster paints, print on the first one: MOTHER GOOSE PARTY; on the second one: PENNY'S BIRTHDAY; on the third one: SATURDAY, OCTOBER 15, 11:30. When dry, deflate the balloons and send by mail. The little girls will have to blow up the balloons in order to find out about the party.

PARTY SCHEDULE

11:30 Children arrive.
11:35 to 12:00 Candy-kiss hunt.
Musical bumps.
Acting out nursery rhymes.
Putting the candles on the cake.
12:00 Grand march to the table and around it led by the birthday child.
12:05 to 12:30 Lunch.

12:30 to 1:00 Quiet games:
Mother Goose quiz.
A story read by the mother.
1:00 to 1:30 Games; old favorites such as:
The Farmer in the Dell.
London Bridge.
Hide the Thimble.
Here We Go 'Round the Mulberry Bush.
Did You Ever See a Lassie?
1:30 Party's over.

PRETTY TABLE

We used a round Extenda-top table over a card table. On this we used a round white cloth topped by a round organdy cloth, white background flocked with pink, blue, and yellow coin dots. The same colors were used for paper plates, mugs and napkins.

White forks and spoons are of plastic.

On the plates are rainbow surprise balls which conceal fifteen small gifts.

Dainty butterflies in various colors, designed to be worn in the hair, are poised on the napkins.

A ring of flickering candles shaped like miniature angel cakes encircles the pedestal cake plate. On this are arranged miniature birthday cakes frosted in pastel colors.

Colored balloons with guests' names painted on them double as place cards and extra favors. Tie one to the back of each chair with pretty ribbon. Clusters of balloons in rainbow hues are placed here and there around the party rooms.

"HOW-TO" SECTION

ANGEL CAKE CANDLES

You will need:

1. Individual angel cake tins which are available now in most kitchenware departments and ten-cent stores.
2. A supply of candle ends or a package or two of paraffin, the kind used for canning.
3. Wax crayons in various colors.
4. A package of "angel chime" candles available in most ten-cent stores.
5. 3 or 4 empty, clean cans for melting wax. Place these in:
6. A kettle of hot water. Keep this at simmer stage on stove. Do not let kettle boil dry.
7. Newspapers to cover working table.

Method:

1. Place candle ends or paraffin in tin cans. Place cans in kettle of hot water to melt. (Warning: *never* heat candle ends or paraffin in pan directly over flame, as they are flammable; always use a pan of boiling water.)
2. Add small pieces of wax crayon to color as desired; when melted, stir together so that color will be even.
3. Pour into angel pans to fill. Place in refrigerator. As the wax hardens, you will have to add a little more melted wax, so be sure you have enough. Otherwise the color will be different.
4. Remove from refrigerator when candles are hard. Allow several hours. Remove from pan. Invert.
5. Set each one on a little piece of cardboard.
6. Holding the candle firmly down against the cardboard, pour a little melted wax in the hole. Hold down until it hardens. Then add a little more each time until it comes within an inch of the top.
7. When wax is almost hard, insert an angel chime candle into the wax in the hole, and hold it upright until the candle is steady.
8. Place candle "cakes" on lacy paper doilies. You will find that these are very easy to make, and fun too. They are very practical as they will burn for hours. Keep them for all family birthday celebrations.

RAINBOW SURPRISE BALLS
For little girls

Assemble fifteen or more small items dear to a little girl's heart. Here are some suggestions: Odd-shaped balloon, tiny powder puff, doll furniture, water flowers, piece of wrapped candy, tiny bottle of perfume, tiny ball and jacks, magnets, tiny figures of animals.

Buy crepe paper in several colors that will harmonize with your color scheme. Cut straight through the folded package in 1-inch strips.

Start with a small ball; wrap, and stretch the paper as you go, turning round and round until the article is covered; then add something else. Every article should be completely covered before you add another. As you come to the end of one strip, choose a different color for the next one. The surprise ball, when completed, will be almost as large as a grapefruit. Tie securely with ribbon of contrasting color.

Each child at the party receives one.

Children open them after refreshments. The work involved in making them will be well worth it when you hear the squeaks and excitement they cause.

Warning: you'll find you're literally wading through crepe paper after the grand opening. But let it go; the myriad rainbow colors lying in piles on the floor add just that much more party atmosphere as far as the children are concerned. Have each little girl put her pile of surprises in a safe place to take home. Small boxes or candy bags would be handy to dole out at this time.

⟨ *Each surprise ball should be a different color on the outside.*

PAPER CHAIN IN RAINBOW COLORS

Prior to the party, the little hostess will have fun making "rainbow chains." These are easy to make and effective as swags on windows and in doorways. To make: Cut construction paper of various colors into strips 6 inches long by ½ inch wide. Staple the ends of the first one together. Loop the second strip through the first one and staple. Continue until you have the desired length. Making rainbow chains might be one of the games for the party.

INSTRUCTIONS FOR MAKING BUTTERFLIES

Lay butterfly pattern on double thickness of coarse crinoline. Trace around pattern, then cut. Paint butterflies in bright colors with poster paint. When dry, insert a pipe cleaner—the colored kind if available—between the thicknesses. (Pipe cleaner has been folded in two to resemble feelers.) With darning wool, sew over and over the body of the butterfly. The front and back sections of the butterfly are then glued together. Trim with sequins or glitter.

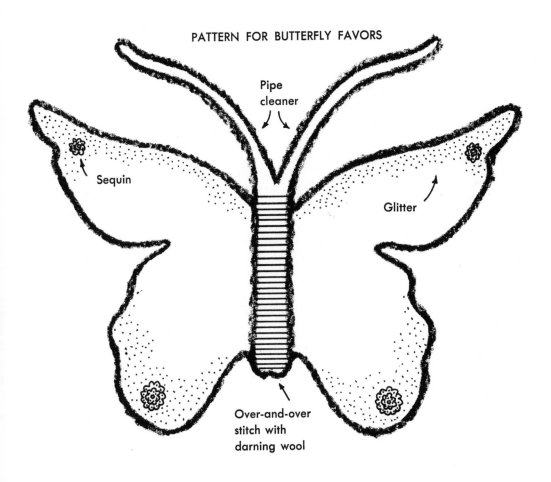

PATTERN FOR BUTTERFLY FAVORS

Pipe cleaner

Sequin

Glitter

Over-and-over stitch with darning wool

FUN TIME

CHINA DOG AND CALICO CAT CANDY-KISS HUNT

Props: One paper bag marked "Kittens," and one bag marked "Doggies"
Twenty-five or thirty candy kisses to hide before the party

This is noisy fun and a good party starter. Mother will have to get in on this one as scorekeeper. Children are divided into two teams, the Three Little Kittens, and the Three Little Doggies. At the signal, all start hunting for the kisses. No team member may pick up a candy kiss. When she finds one, she must either mew or bark until Mother gets to her. Mother then puts the kiss into either the kitten bag or the doggie bag, depending on who finds the kisses. At the end of ten minutes, kisses are counted. Each member of the winning team selects a prize from the table. Then each of the remaining children selects a prize. (You can't lose at this party!)

PUTTING THE CANDLES ON THE CAKE

Props: A large piece of paper on which a birthday cake is drawn.
Crayons.

Each child has a different colored crayon. Children are blindfolded in turn and asked to draw three candles on the cake.

MOTHER GOOSE QUIZ

Children as well as adults love quizzes; try this and see.

Children are divided into two teams again, the Kittens and the Doggies. They sit facing one another, and Mother or some other adult asks questions of first one side and then the other.

Sample questions:

What did the Three Little Kittens lose?

Whom did Little Red Riding Hood visit?

Where did Peter Peter Pumpkin Eater put his wife?

How many fiddlers did Old King Cole have?

Who put the kettle on?

What ran up the clock?

Better assemble a good supply of questions. They'll want to play this for quite a while.

ACTING OUT NURSERY RHYMES

Another fascinating Mother Goose pastime is for all the children to recite or sing familiar nursery rhymes and act them out at the same time; for example:

Jack and Jill went up the hill (point up)
To fetch a pail of water (pick up imaginary pail)
Jack fell down (all fall down)
And broke his crown (pat top of head)
And Jill came tumbling after (make tumbling motion with hands).

Additional suggestions for nursery rhymes to act out:

Little Jack Horner
Little Boy Blue
Little Miss Muffet
Rock-a-bye Baby
Old Woman in the Shoe

OLD FAVORITES

Play each of the following games for five minutes. In this way, the children will not tire of any of them.

The Farmer in the Dell
London Bridge
Hide the Thimble
Here We Go Round the Mulberry Bush
Did You Ever See a Lassie?

MUSICAL BUMPS

Children skip or walk around in a circle in time to the music. When the music stops, they all drop to the floor. Last one down each time drops out of the game. This continues until one player is left. She gets first choice of prizes on the table; then the others each choose one.

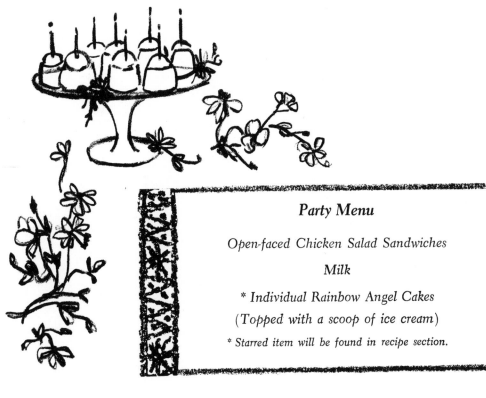

Party Menu

Open-faced Chicken Salad Sandwiches

Milk

* Individual Rainbow Angel Cakes

(Topped with a scoop of ice cream)

* Starred item will be found in recipe section.

RAINBOW ANGEL CAKES

Prepare 1 pkg. angel food mix according to directions on package.

Using 'individual angel cake pans, bake 10 minutes less than if it were a large cake.

Invert pan, cool, and remove from pan.

Frosting

1 pkg. confectioners' sugar

Enough hot water to make an icing just thin enough to pour

Divide into four portions.

Color one portion pink, one yellow, one green, one lilac, or colors of your own choice.

Pour the icing slowly over the cakes, letting some dribble down inside, and some dribble down the sides of the cakes—as if you were icing petit-fours.

When the icing becomes firm, place each cake on a paper doily. Arrange cakes on a pedestal cake plate, tucking fresh posies here and there. Use as a centerpiece.

TO SERVE

Just before dessert time, remove to kitchen, and put a small scoop of ice cream on top of each cake. In the ice cream, place one birthday candle. Light the candles and bring cakes to the table to the strains of "Happy Birthday to You."

When each child is served, ask her to make a wish. At the signal, each blows out her own candle.

bibliography

I highly recommend the following books.

ON PARTIES IN GENERAL

Successful Entertaining in Your Home, Carolyn Coggins, Prentice-Hall, Inc., Englewood Cliffs, New Jersey, 1952.

Entertaining Is Fun, Dorothy Draper, Doubleday & Company, Inc., New York, 1945.

The Perfect Hostess, Maureen Daly, Dodd, Mead & Company, Inc., New York, 1950.

The Hostess Manual, Marguerite Kohl and Frederica Young, David McKay Company, Inc., New York, 1954.

Home Entertaining, Charlotte Adams, Crown Publishers, Inc., New York.

Cokesbury Party Book, Arthur Depew, Cokesbury Press, Nashville, Tennessee, 1932.

Party and Crafts Books, Dennison Mfg. Co., New York.

R.S.V.P., Toni Taylor, Thomas Y. Crowell Company, New York, 1937.

MY FAVORITE COOK BOOKS

Betty Crocker's Picture Cook Book, McGraw-Hill Book Company, Inc., New York, 1956.

Good Housekeeping Cook Book, edited by Dorothy B. Marsh, Rinehart & Company, Inc., New York, rev. ed., 1955.

Better Homes and Gardens Cook Book, Meredith Publishing Co., Des Moines, Iowa, 3d ed.

A Cook's Tour of Quantico, privately published by the Officers' Wives Garden Club, Marine Corps Schools, Quantico, Virginia, 1952.

Gourmet Cook Book, Gourmet Distributing Corp., New York, rev. ed., 1956.

Thoughts for Food, Houghton Mifflin Company, Boston, 1946.

One Arm Cookery, Mary Lasswell, Houghton Mifflin Company, Boston, 1946.

Shrimp Cookery, Helen Worth, The Citadel Press, New York, 1952.

ETIQUETTE BOOKS

Complete Book of Etiquette, Amy Vanderbilt, Doubleday & Company, Inc., New York, rev. ed., 1956.

Etiquette, Emily Post, Funk & Wagnalls Company, New York, 9th ed., 1955.

GAME BOOKS

Party Games, Maggi McNellis and Hubie Boscowitz, Prentice-Hall, Inc., Englewood Cliffs, New Jersey, 1949.

101 Best Party Games for Adults, Lillian and Godfrey Frankel, Sterling Publ., New York, 1954.

Social Games for Recreation, Bernard S. Mason and Elmer D. Mitchell, A. S. Barnes and Company, New York, 1935.

The Book of Games and Parties, Theresa Hunt Wolcott, Small Maynard and Co., 1920.

About the Author

Mrs. Brent has had years of experience as a gracious hostess. "I can't remember the time," she says, "that I wasn't interested in parties. My mother and father were the perfect hostess and host, never happier than when the house was full of people. My love for beautiful table settings began as a young girl when my family started for me a collection of lovely English bone china cups and saucers." As the wife of a Marine Corps colonel, Mrs. Brent has lived on posts from Quantico, Va., to Guam, always collecting and trying out new party ideas and menus. To help coordinate the details of successful party giving, she developed the Party Plan, which is both a blueprint and a timetable for the hostess. Mrs. Brent has given a course in table decoration and informal entertainment and has written a number of magazine articles on parties and entertaining.